To the spirit of

Frances Davison Cheney

Who made George Stacey possible

With warm appreciation forever for

Anne Cheney Zinsser

Who made this book possible

With love to Thong Nguyen

George Stacey

and the Creation of
AMERICAN CHIC

Maureen Footer

RIZZOLI
NEW YORK

New York · Paris · London · Milan

Foreword by **MARIO BUATTA**

CONTENTS

George Stacey and Babe Paley antiquing in Paris

The Fellow Had Pizzazz

—Mario Buatta

I was 23 and a design assistant at B. Altman and Company—I didn't have my style yet, but I did know I loved my aunt's chintzes—when I discovered George Stacey. I saw the Levy house in *Vogue* and was completely bowled over. I was amazed when I saw what he did. The symmetry, the placement, the contrast, the quality of light, the casual use of antiques. This guy had *pizzazz*.

A few years later, I saw more of Stacey's work in *The Finest Rooms by America's Great Decorators*. I couldn't stop looking at those pictures, either. He had an incredible color sense, the ability to mix genres and periods seamlessly, a talent for intimate seating arrangements, and a perfect sense of scale and proportion. Most of all, his flair for arranging objects and paintings was unparalleled, and it was this that had a direct influence on me. By then, I had a new apartment and had also acquired my first dog paintings and Staffordshire dogs—and brackets, too, of course. Inspired by Stacey's wall arrangements and with Stanley Barrows [the director of the interior design department at Parsons School of Design from 1946 to 1968] egging me on, I experimented with a composition of paintings, brackets, Staffordshire dogs, and bows. I thought I'd landed on something. To this very day, I have George Stacey in mind every time I create a wall composition. He was the master of placement.

It seems to me that today people don't seem to know what to do with space. Stacey had a wonderful classic system of organizing a room that still works. With Stacey there was structure to the rooms, and then he would lighten it up. In the same way, he also brought a European—mostly French—accent to his work. But he did it in an offhand American way. His use of architecture was also easy and unforced. Stacey's recessed arch-shaped bookcases for Thomas Guinzburg (also featured in *The Finest Rooms*) inspired not just a few rooms for my clients; I reinterpreted them in my own living room, too.

I eventually met Stacey through my client Gates Davison, whose family lent Stacey the squash court that he adapted into a weekend house. I was in Europe, and Davison had been in Russia with Lilly Phipps. We met up in Paris and drove out to Houdan to see Stacey at Le Poulailler. We sat out on the terrace and talked. The decorator I so respected turned out to be quite a character. He reminded me of Monsieur Hulot from the movie *Monsieur Hulot's Holiday*. And he smoked that cigarette with a little holder and wore a hat all the time. I had to tell him how much I admired his work.

He was a wonderful classicist. Look at his own apartment—it's great, it's glamorous. When people have absorbed the classical principles of design, they can twist the rules and do something new. Stacey did that with confidence before others even knew the rules. When it is right, as it was with Stacey, it looks effortless and light and modern. The colors are lovely. He had a great sense of style. And the lessons are timeless. I know—I am still using them.

Both the elegantly recessed bookcase and the dazzling display of paintings and porcelain in Mario Buatta's own living room bear witness to the influence of George Stacey.

The Messenger of Modern

With the 1934 completion of his first commission, an art deco octagonal house on Long Island, George Stacey charted a new direction in American design. America was entering its prime, newly confident and ready for a style that reflected its recently acquired sophistication and independence from strict European models. Stacey, a young man from Connecticut via Paris, channeled the influences that shaped the new mind-set: the abundance of the 1920s and the worldliness, cultural access, and discernment that accompanied wealth; the inquisitiveness of an arriving world power; and the darker reality of the 1930s (his own Paris-based antiques business had floundered). Sifting these elements with a nonchalance worthy of Cole Porter, Stacey created designs that perfectly expressed the new mood—and engendered a new, quintessential American style, one that was to alter the course of design in this country.

Stacey had created chic as no one had done before, banishing overburdened, overworked richness and instead conjuring light and dark, form and profile, Steuben crystal and klismos chairs, silk and a soupçon of French furniture into a light and lilting art deco sensation that captured the insouciance, worldliness, and confidence of an ebullient society girl. Soon, other tastemakers and trendsetters of the highest order were clamoring for Stacey's blend of dash and sophistication: Diana Vreeland, fashion editor extraordinaire; Babe Paley, Betsey Roosevelt Whitney, and Minnie Astor, the celebrated Cushing sisters; Brenda Diana Duff Frazier, debutante of the century; captains of industry, diplomats, and statesmen Bill Paley, Vincent Astor, Jock Whitney,

and Averell Harriman; philanthropist Anthony Drexel Duke; publisher Harold Guinzburg; and Hollywood powerhouses Ava Gardner and Grace Kelly. As Stacey calibrated his designs to reflect each client and the prevailing mood, his work distilled time, place, and individual into distinctive, of-the-moment rooms.

Given his fashionable clients and eclectic, confident style, it was inevitable that Stacey would become a media darling. Editors at *Vogue, Town & Country, House & Garden,* and *Harper's Bazaar* avidly published his inventive rooms, which injected classic training with cool irreverence and au courant glamour. Diana Vreeland, as always, went one step further: *she* staged fashion shoots with her grandest photographers against these dazzling backdrops. The results were mesmerizing.

As Stacey mapped the template for timeless, breezy design, colleagues also took note. Billy Baldwin would extend the Stacey aesthetic with his own pared-down, clear-colored designs. Stacey's designs anticipated the great years of Sister Parish, with her emphasis on sensual comfort and eclecticism. In the 1960s, Michael Taylor echoed, nearly verbatim, aspects of Stacey in fabulous rooms on the West Coast. Mark Hampton paid tribute to Stacey in writing and in kind: his neoclassical cocoa-colored living room punctuated with white

A kaleidoscope of color, historicism, romance, and reason: when the author interpreted the work of Stacey in a twenty-first-century room, the results were stylish and timeless. Stacey's designs in the 1930s introduced modern principles to American design.

was the aesthetic successor to a smart Stacey salon in Bermuda that had appeared in *Vogue* in 1947. Stacey's talent for color, scale, and wall composition—as well as signature inset bookcases—provided Mario Buatta with ongoing inspiration for client designs, as well as for his own apartments. Stanley Barrows, the late dean of interior design at the Parsons School of Design, encouraged students to study Stacey for his brilliant jewel palettes and for lost lessons on discipline and spontaneity, glamour and sobriety, antiques and improvised elements. Wittingly or not, modern designers working in such disparate venues as the White House, Lyford Cay, and Gstaad incorporate the cosmopolitan legacy of Stacey into their designs. The Stacey blend of historicism, connoisseurship, modernity, and superb placement remains the foundation for rooms of character and staying power.

Despite the accolades and glamour, Stacey the man remained something of a mystery. As most of his projects developed quietly through an enviable network of fashionable women and prominent leaders (many of them Skull and Bones men), the introverted

Stacey didn't seek or need the spotlight. Unlike William Pahlmann and Billy Baldwin, Stacey did not write a book that would encapsulate his career into a design reference volume. And while prescient decorators, such as Eleanor McMillen Brown, established firms that continued their legacies and carried their names into the next century, Stacey simply shuttered his business upon retirement. As a result, while Stacey's influence is evident in the work of just about every designer, George Stacey himself became elusive.

Over the years, those interested in design history have had tantalizing but brief encounters with Stacey's work. A breezily chic Palm Beach house, a tranquil château in France, and the most inviting library-cum-living room—all by Stacey—can be found in the iconic design book *The Finest Rooms*. After a thirty-year dearth of information, a profile of Stacey by Mark Hampton appeared in *House & Garden* in 1993, but little else would follow. Drawn to Stacey's Franco-American aesthetic, I grasped every fragment of information to appear on Stacey. Finally, when engaged to design a model apartment using Grace Kelly (a Stacey client) as muse, I had the opportunity to experiment with applying Stacey's design tenets to modern living. The result was an effortlessly classic apartment that left me in spellbound admiration for this beguiling but obscure designer. It also begged then unanswerable questions: Who was this mysterious man born in the era of Teddy Roosevelt whose work lent itself—and continues to lend itself—so easily to a modern point of view? What forces shaped his innovative eye? Above all, what lessons can we glean from Stacey to create surroundings that are more chic, more timeless, more beautiful today and tomorrow?

Researching these answers unveiled a compelling story—and the rediscovery of a master. William Odom and Frank Alvah Parsons, Stacey's two great mentors, surely would have answered that rigorous study of classical design affords the freedom to reinterpret in an elegant and relevant manner. Stacey, of course, did exactly that. Although Stacey's world was one populated by gilt-wood mirrors and Coromandel screens, pedestals and urns, satin and damask, lacquer, fanciful girandoles, and columns, his work was a deft mix of high design and the everyday. Stacey balanced his iconoclastic color palettes and romantic tendencies with disciplined classicism. Possessing a trained eye that invariably selected that which was beautifully conceived and enduring,

Stacey blended art deco elements with baroque *objets* and modular seating. His passion, French furniture, was well evident in his designs, but he used it with offhand ease: it found its way into rooms that could be humble as well as grand, and it no longer sat in state in formal period rooms. Instead, in a Stacey interior, a Migeon commode could easily be found next to a moderne chair, comfortable upholstery, and a Chinese lacquer hatbox. At will, and given his classical base, Stacey neatly dispensed with convention—mingling rattan picnic chairs with blackamoors, fashioning a cachepot from a salad bowl—to provide the note of daring that Stacey client Diana Vreeland famously described as "pizzazz."

Vreeland rightly might have added that the key to Stacey style was her maxim "Elegance is refusal." It was this refusal that lent his rooms chic. While Stacey's vision was essentially a luxurious one, he was at heart a disciplined stylist who gave way to whimsy but never indulgence in his rooms. Throughout his life, he retained traces of his Connecticut roots, which imparted a discernible American inflection to his work: a typical Stacey room was slightly spare, always rational, and never too serious. Stacey's rooms—even those that border on the baroque—are balanced, beautifully arranged, and poised, exhibiting an elegant understatement, an ability to edit, and, when necessary, Yankee ingenuity.

In the end, however, the power of a Stacey room defied categorization and formula, as its beauty was attributable to Stacey's individual gift for the intangible elements of design: an intuitive understanding of the power of light and shadow, profile and scale, glamour and reality, romance and melancholy, and constant synchronization with his extraordinary clients. This visual acuity—poetry, in fact—may have been the result of a profound sense of isolation. Behind a stylized exterior of black clothes, perpetual cigarette, laconic wit, and luxury cars, behind Stacey's handsome residences, ranging from a Louis XIII château to urbane apartments in New York and Paris to a converted squash court on Long Island and a former henhouse in the French countryside, was a reserved and complex man who knew not only success and great friendships but also private pain. Beauty was the palliative. Composing, maintaining, arranging, and fine-tuning beautiful objects and interiors were constant preoccupations. Even when Stacey was in his nineties, colleagues would see him meandering along 57th Street—a frail man in a black coat peering into antique-store windows, still ferreting out the most refined and elegant neoclassical objects, searching for the item that would fill the proverbial void. Arbiters of taste, however, saw it quite another way: Stacey had years ago addressed the chasm in American design. Departing from complacent acceptance of both European and vernacular design standards—indeed of *any* dogmatic design aesthetic—Stacey established a design vocabulary for a country in search of its own sophisticated style. His design work reflected in its prism the American ascendancy in its golden age. In doing so, he defined American chic in the American Century, and his legacy endures, glitteringly, to this day.

T*hough classical principles grounded any Stacey interior, the decorator also raffishly bent the rules. In his East Side apartment (opposite), he incorporated personal mementos in a gilt-framed grouping. In the salon of his château in the Île-de-France (below), he mismatched curtains with impunity.*

CHAPTER ONE

ORIGINS OF AN AESTHETE

1066–1920

In a smart twist of fate, George Stacey, an adventurer in French style, descended from Gallic daredevil Eustace II, Count of Boulogne. Elegantly gesturing and galloping in perpetuity on the Bayeux Tapestry, the Count became the stuff of legend by delivering the grisly coup de grâce at the Battle of Hastings. Afterward, as a member of William the Conqueror's inner circle, he proceeded to establish himself on English soil, though he later fell from grace due to some self-serving maneuvering in Kent. Over time, his descendants Anglicized their name from Eustace to Stacy (the *e* came later with greater aspirations), slipped from ruling to working class, and existed without notable incident for eight centuries in Yorkshire.

If George Stacey had been aware of his aristocratic, albeit distant, French lineage, he might have worn a signet ring—a bona fide one, too, as the count's crest is probably the only one accurately depicted on the Bayeux Tapestry (not surprisingly as the tapestry is thought to have been commissioned by the count to regain favor with the king). Certainly in Stacey's time, fashionable

Although born into austere New England circumstances, Stacey possessed natural flair that may be traced to a flamboyant French ancestor, Eustace II, Count of Boulogne. The Bayeux Tapestry depicts the count (second from left), a member of William the Conqueror's inner circle, grandiloquently gesturing toward the king, wearing full—and accurately rendered—armorial regalia. While the colorful count delivered the coup de grâce at the Battle of Hastings, he later committed an act of treason; reportedly, he then commissioned the Bayeux Tapestry to restore his favor with the king. His English descendants Anglicized the family name Eustace to Stacy. George Stacey's genetic predisposition for the dramatic was neatly counterbalanced by Yankee understatement.

men-about-town such as Nicky de Gunzburg wore such rings quite dashingly, but Stacey was too restrained and too uncertain for showy embellishment. Nevertheless, nearly a thousand years after the Norman conquest, Stacey retained the family gene for the grand French gesture, albeit of a more domestic nature.

If George was understated by choice, his forebears were unpretentious by circumstance. By 1849, ancestral pride was irrelevant as the Stacys faced the grim reality of Sheffield, England, a town caught in the upheaval of the Industrial Revolution. For simple knife makers such as the Stacys, if there was to be a future it would have to be found elsewhere. Across the ocean, Connecticut beckoned, promising a second chance. By 1850, the burgeoning manufacturing powerhouse counted more factory workers than farmers, and its knife-making, foundry, and arms industries drew heavily upon Sheffield for skilled labor. But despite great promise, the Stacys' American beginnings were inauspicious.

Foreshadowing the family's forever shaky foothold in the New World, George Stacey's grandfather wasn't born securely on terra firma but precariously in steerage class to a lone woman crossing the Atlantic. Upon landing, Ann Stacy and the new infant made their way to Southington, Connecticut, where her husband, James Stacy, had already found work as a battery polisher. While other immigrant boys in nineteenth-century America struck out on their own with ambitions and grand visions to become the stuff of American lore, John Stacy, the boy born ominously at sea, squelched any family hopes for advancement by becoming a humble cutler like his Sheffield ancestors. In 1880, John's wife, Eliza, gave birth to George's father, Alford Stacy, a dreamer who would add the more elegant *e* to the family name.

Not long after the Stacys' arrival, the linking of the transcontinental railroad in 1869 ignited a new era of growth and wealth in America, an important prelude to George Stacey's aesthetic development. Access to new resources, markets, and opportunities, as well as financial speculation, provided the foundation for spectacular new fortunes. As freshly minted millionaires required appropriate status symbols—and, of all the trappings of wealth, houses were the most personal reflection of money, taste, culture, and position—domestic architecture changed dramatically. Naturally, American financiers and industrialists looked to established European traditions for models, especially the architecture of the French Second Empire—a dizzying and often incoherent combination of gothic, Italianate, and eighteenth-century French elements. For interiors, French firms, especially that of Jules Allard, buoyed by the favor of architect-tastemakers Horace Trumbauer and Stanford White (who commissioned Allard to decorate his own house in Gramercy Square), were frequently favored. When Allard supplied the French salon for William Kissam Vanderbilt's Fifth Avenue house in 1883, Mrs. Vanderbilt scored a major social coup: the haughty Mrs. Astor was compelled to call on her arriviste rival to ensure her daughter an invitation to dance in the celebrated room. Effectively, lavish French interiors became mandatory for many an aspiring hostess.

Once completed, these elaborate rooms were filled with treasures from the Old World. American accumulation of such riches became even easier after England imposed death duties in 1894, which induced old families to break up their great estates, engendering fire sales of art, antiques, and property. J. P. Morgan most notably availed himself of the spoils of the new tax duties as well as the 1909 Payne-Aldrich Tariff Act, which exempted art and antiques from import duties, but in fact everyone who was anyone seemed to own a Rembrandt. Nevertheless, despite the presence of some fine paintings and antiques, interiors in the Gilded Age were largely a florid and cumbersome lot.

It was not a moment for understated elegance. Like membership on Mrs. Astor's Four Hundred list, the standard for good taste was arbitrary, a matter of ownership rather than aesthetics. Ostentation conveniently conveyed position within a constantly shifting social pyramid. Accordingly, expense was not a consideration but an asset, further discouraging any attempts at restraint. The ballroom at the Marble House in Newport, covered in twenty-two-karat gold leaf, triumphed above all in the game of conspicuous consumption: its cost

C oupled with the extravagance of the Gilded Age, the natural exuberance of American architect Stanford White produced interiors of extreme richness. A few decades later, Stacey and others would counteract this trend with sleek glamour and moderne trappings. Like White, Stacey was an incurable collector and passionate assembler of beautiful things, so his version of modern interiors was noteworthy for antiques of broad provenance incorporated into clean settings.

twinkled showily on the surface long after the French master craftsmen departed.

An inevitable reaction to the prevailing taste, with its loss of restraint, preponderance of surface decoration, lack of proportion, and decline in craftsmanship, began to ferment. While some championed the Arts and Crafts movement for aesthetic as well as moral redemption, others looked to classicism for answers. In 1897, Edith Wharton and architect Ogden Codman Jr.

*I*n the nineteenth century, expense was not a consideration; in fact, it was perceived as an asset. The ballroom at the Marble House (preceding page) in Newport trumped all in the game of conspicuous consumption: it was covered in twenty-two-karat gold leaf. The cost twinkled showily on the surface long after the master craftsmen brought over at great expense returned to France.

Before Edith Wharton, a model of decorum in velvet gown and ropes of pearls (below), documented a society in transition in closely observed novels, she teamed with architect Ogden Codman Jr. to write The Decoration of Houses. *The treatise, published in 1897, lobbied for the return of classical principles and reason in design and pushed the aesthetic pendulum toward elegant restraint.*

published *The Decoration of Houses*, drawing a line in the sand for good taste. Advocating sixteenth-century Italian architecture and its offspring (particularly the work of Inigo Jones in England and the Louis XIV style in France), reason, and restraint, the authors sketched an outline for elegant, relatively reductive design at the dawn of the twentieth century.

Also early in the twentieth century, but light-years away from the Newport cottages and Fifth Avenue mansions parsed by Wharton and Codman, George Stacey grew up in Stratford, Connecticut, an insular town engaged in agriculture and oyster farming on Long Island Sound. His father, Alford Stacey, had moved to Stratford in 1899, where town records show he was employed as a clerk. At the turn of the century, when Stacey was born, the pastoral town had giant wine-glass elms lining grassy streets, freshly painted gabled houses, a town green, the requisite Congregational church, a single schoolhouse, and milestones set by Benjamin Franklin when he was postmaster general. As it had been since Colonial times, Stratford was still governed by town selectmen, but like many institutions at the beginning of the twentieth century, it hovered on the cusp of change.

Unlike his father, who continued in the same trade as his grandfather, Alford Stacey came to Stratford with hopes of becoming an engineer. A recent connection by trolley line to neighboring, industrial Bridgeport generated new prosperity and a flurry of construction in Stratford. Propitiously, Alford married Belle Bennett Morehouse, whose father was a civil engineer. Although Alford and Belle were both members of Christ Episcopal Church, their marriage is not recorded in the church registry, only in Stratford town hall records, suggesting that the young couple eloped. As a clandestine, secular marriage was an unusual occurrence in a small, close-knit town in 1900, it appears the respectable Morehouses did not approve of the unproven newcomer of little background.

It was an unlikely but explainable marriage that seemed to totter indefinitely. For Alford, the marriage represented a step up the socio-economic ladder. By linking himself with the more established Morehouse clan, who claimed both a granite obelisk showily marking their family burial plot and, later, a street bearing their name, Alford gained a foothold in the professional class. For her part, Belle sustained a seemingly prickly relationship with her stepmother and half sisters and

probably looked to marriage with an aspiring professional as a means to escape her family while maintaining the prerogatives of the small-town bourgeoisie.

Though twenty-one-year-old Alford Stacey wistfully described his occupation as "engineer" on his son's birth certificate on December 11, 1901, Alford's youthful dream never materialized; instead, patchy employment records show Alford Stacey holding a series of unspecialized short-lived jobs (ice dealer, lumber clerk, oyster salesman) that would justify a father-in-law's disapproval and garner a wife's disappointment. Most likely, it was only through his civically prominent father-in-law's intercession (William Morehouse eventually became the town engineer) that Alford obtained several municipal posts; in addition to tree warden for Stratford's prize wine-glass elms, he was at various times town truant officer and constable. One can easily imagine a tense, insecure household.

Whereas Alford was impractical but sociable, amiably participating in church activities and joining the local Masonic order, George was the opposite of his father—talented and awkward—and didn't fit into Stratford's rhythms. Instead, he was a tentative loner, teased by his classmates for his effeminacy and hopelessness with girls. In the high school record book, *The Centennial*, George was censoriously voted "Most

Twenty-one when his son, George, was born, Alford Stacey *(above, left) harbored dreams of becoming an engineer; in reality, he held a string of odd jobs (from truant officer to oyster salesman) and attempted his own business selling ice, firewood, and domestic lumber. When he died in 1933, Stacey père owned little aside from twenty worthless shares of Fox Theatres common stock, a fatality of the Great Crash. Characteristics in his son were inversed: whereas Alford was hapless but outgoing, George was clever but painfully shy.*

Stacey's mother was part of the bourgeois Morehouse clan of Stratford, Connecticut. Belle Bennett Morehouse Stacey signaled estrangement from her family by eschewing the obelisk-embellished family burial plot for a simple gravestone near friends. George, a devotee of houses from a young age, retained a sentimental attachment to his mother's family house and kept a photo of it among his papers to the end of his life (above, right). The home's breezy casualness would echo in Stacey's future work for Diana Vreeland and others.

Girly Boy" by his classmates as well as mocked for his assumption of long pants (the 1916 outward sign of manhood). In later years, George's lifelong lack of confidence was disguised by a laconic reserve, and his shyness transformed itself into a concise, often acerbic, wit. But before he developed the protective shell of an adult persona, being the odd man out in a class of eighteen could only have hurt.

There was little in Stratford to help George Stacey find his stride. His family's chronic lack of money prevented George from partaking in youthful entertainments that might have fostered friendships, such as picnics, hayrides, and outings to Lordship Beach. Perhaps in a clumsy attempt to boost his socially foundering son, the endearing Alford Stacey purchased ads for his struggling domestic lumber and ice business in the high school bulletin—as if teenagers would be likely customers for a household staple. And while Belle apparently shared George's interest in European culture, not only did the tight financial situation keep this mutual interest at bay, but George and his mother also appear to have been emotionally remote from each other. Although she lived until George was in his fifties, even his closest friends—if they knew about his mother at all—knew virtually nothing about her.

Beauty became a refuge for George Stacey, and drawing houses, especially the grander ones in Stratford, a frequent diversion. To the end of his days, Stacey spoke of a particular sea captain's house with a barometer in the newel post that he had loved to draw. The library in the center of town provided another oasis with books on art, architecture, decorative arts, and Europe, subjects that enticed Stacey to the end of his life. This early pursuit of architecture and connoisseurship developed into a lifelong pattern, a practice that unfailingly absorbed Stacey and defined him. Whenever he was browsing among Left Bank *antiquaires* with Babe Paley (who, like George, found solace in antiquing), furnishing his Louis XIII château object by object, or chitchatting with fellow decorators about recent finds, Stacey was always confident and at his best.

Notwithstanding Stacey's attraction to beauty and his copious drawing, the notion of his leaving Stratford to attend design school could only have been considered preposterous in 1919. At the time, it was unusual for young residents to stray from the leafy confines of Stratford. Most high school graduates remained in town,

often entering family businesses, or found employment in neighboring Bridgeport, which had prospered with munitions contracts during World War I. (Only three students who were graduated from Stratford High School in 1917 left town to attend college, while a fourth volunteered in France during World War I—and returned to Stratford to operate a gas station decorated with patriotic war memorabilia.) Even more concrete an obstacle was the lack of money—the cost of tuition alone made the notion unthinkable for a family like the Staceys. With little hope of translating dreamy aspirations into a practical plan, it was fortunate for George that a perceptive and pragmatic teacher arrived on the scene. After sizing up George's talent for drawing, his financial situation, and perhaps his alienation, the newly arrived English teacher Violet Kutcher wrote to the New York School of Fine and Applied Art (later the legendary Parsons School of Design) for an application on George's behalf. All that drawing must have evidenced significant talent, for Stacey was awarded a scholarship, something Frank Alvah Parsons conferred only very selectively.

Over the years, as renown and legend accumulated, fashionable, slightly distant decorator George Stacey, with a château in France and a patrician bearing, was rumored to have rebelled both against joining the family's established lumber business and a long family tradition of attending Yale to pursue his passion for design. As Yale archives, however, show no hapless Staceys or Stacys (or Morehouses or Bennetts, for that matter) in university records for the relevant years, George was probably the first Stacey to obtain any higher education. At age eighteen, in 1919, Stacey moved to New York to attend design school on the Upper West Side. As for many curious minds, design school was but the beginning of a larger education. Studies of art and architecture fostered an appreciation of history, the opportunity to live in Paris (and master the French language), acquisition of objects, and a broad range of acquaintances in the arts and affairs. Via this introduction to aesthetics, Stacey's mind was attuned and made receptive to ideas that would in turn shape his work.

Other factors besides sympathetic English teachers converged to create an environment hospitable to the ascendance of Stacey's star. The year of his birth, 1901, coincided with the start of the presidency of Theodore Roosevelt and the accession of Edward VII, men instrumental in the formation of the modern world. Under

Roosevelt, attention in America shifted outward to foreign policy. Concurrently, Edward VII bound Europe with alliances under the Entente Cordiale, unwittingly putting into play forces that would lead to World War I. America's intervention in the war was transformative: not only did the country catch a glimpse of the pivotal role it could play on the international stage, but the war had also opened up its cultural sightlines. Inevitably, as society became more confident, worldly, and curious, its sophistication grew and its design choices would become more independent.

How America lived, and the houses it lived in, continued to evolve as new technologies reshaped the patterns of daily life. With railroads now connecting metropolitan areas and the advent of the car and the telephone for immediate communication, industrialists and financiers began building Georgian and Colonial houses in idyllic enclaves near town for easy weekend escapes. Some even commuted daily into the city by private railroad car, yacht, or automobile. These exurban

Across Long Island Sound from Stratford, Connecticut—where Stacey was growing up in constrained circumstances—Wall Street titans built gracious country homes that departed from the heavy residential commissions of previous decades. In 1914 in Locust Valley, J. P. Morgan partner Henry P. Davison built Peacock Point, which included a Georgian-style house, a casino, a polo field, and an innovative landing strip on seventy-seven acres. Upon marrying, Davison's children would in turn build houses on the sprawling compound. Through Davison's stylish daughter Frances Cheney, Peacock Point would become the locus of Stacey's highly publicized first decorating commission.

I n the dining room of Henry Davison's Peacock Point (above), measured
English sobriety replaced the lavish embellishment of the preceding decades.
Chippendale needlepoint fire screens, inset-fringed chairs, smart half-shield chandelier
shades, Adam candelabra, and urn knife boxes were assembled according to Elsie
de Wolfe's credo of "suitability, simplicity, and proportion." In the warm season,
the chairs were slipcovered in a floral cretonne. Kate Trubee Davison, an avid card
player, spent hours playing canasta at the Georgian concertina table.

The breakfast room at Peacock Point (opposite) was unexpectedly stylized.
Plants and giant plaster floral reliefs lent the room a sunny aspect.

Blending exoticism and experimentation, Henri Matisse's *Orientalist paintings reflected the cosmopolitan spirit reigning in post–World War I Paris, where Matisse, Pablo Picasso, Coco Chanel, André Gide, Jean-Michel Frank, and Josephine Baker shifted the boundaries of convention. In the 1920s, prosperity, a new sense of prominence on the world stage, and shifts in immigration laws prompted Americans to travel, and in doing so they encountered new art forms and observed emerging trends.*

houses, vaguely reminiscent of English country houses, dictated a new way of life, at once urbane and sporting. While still formal, the new houses were less imposing and more self-assured than their Beaux-Arts predecessors. Typical of this building activity was Peacock Point, the 1914 Georgian house that Henry P. Davison, the protégé of J. P. Morgan, built on seventy-seven acres overlooking Long Island Sound. Davison hired Walker and Gillette, architects for Astors and Vanderbilts (as well as the later Parke-Bernet and Fuller buildings in New York), to design the house and engaged Duveen Brothers to assemble his art collection. It was still notably a time of dark old master paintings—Davison reputedly had the requisite Rembrandt—and hushed interiors, but a trend toward the gracious rather than the grand began to take hold and would gain momentum as the century progressed.

Two figures in the decorative arts—William Odom and Elsie de Wolfe—who promoted alternatives to ponderous design defined the field Stacey would initially encounter. Through celebrated students (Stacey among them), selections of antiques, and writing, Odom's understated neoclassical taste reverberates in design to this day. Odom, a pivotal member of the faculty at the New York School of Fine and Applied Art, advocated cerebral, reductive, elegant, and poised interiors. His colors were muted, his placement unparalleled, his objects exquisitely refined. His sobriquet was Mr. Taste. Touring Italy and France with students every summer until the outbreak of war, Odom, like Wharton and Codman, maintained the superiority of Italian Renaissance and eighteenth-century French design. These were the models he made sure his students would experience directly, sketch, and emulate. An active business of antique procurement abroad for prominent New York designers ensured that his taste made its way into some of the best houses in America. After assisting in the collection of antiques for James Deering's fantastical house, Vizcaya, Odom published the two-volume *A History of Italian Furniture* in 1919, to this day the classic English-language reference on Italian antiques.

The retired actress Elsie de Wolfe took a less academic approach to design. In her persuasive *The House in Good Taste* (written with Ruby Ross Wood), de Wolfe argued for what we would now call Edwardian taste—the use of softer pastel walls and white woodwork, bright chintzes for curtains and upholstery, Colonial and European (particularly French) styles, and lots and lots of painted furniture, porcelain bowls, flowers, and knickknacks to enhance a room. Keenly in tune with the new houses and new way of life, she created livable, rather than mere showpiece, rooms, and to this end little was sacred. If necessary, she would use more functional reproduction furniture rather than have wobbly antiques compromise the well-being of a room. Although her warm style evolved to become increasingly spectacular over the years, what mattered most about a de Wolfe room was that it was charming and highly personal.

Stacey would naturally respond to the themes established by Odom and de Wolfe; unfussy taste was practically his birthright. Though he very rarely returned to Stratford, New England had informed Stacey indelibly. An inherent discipline imbues Stacey's work, lending a stylish modernity to the Stacey room, typically filled with French antiques and brilliant colors. Like Stacey's characteristic concise speaking style, his designs have an understatement and organization that offer visual respite amidst the lacquer, urns, carving, and gilding that populate his rooms. And just as Stacey would never have worn anything as extraneous as a ring, his rooms, no matter how embellished, never crossed the line into excess or pretense. In fact, though he is associated with sumptuous satins, silks, and damasks (what *House & Garden* copywriters referred to as "his palace fabrics") and certainly used them for his grand residential and palace projects, if the occasion warranted Yankee thrift, Stacey could quite happily employ inexpensive cottons—or improvise a cachepot from a salad bowl.

As taste became more fluid, it also absorbed broader influences. From the same wellspring that produced political, financial, moral, demographic, and aesthetic change, artistic ideas and images flowed after the war, too. Artists such as Henri Matisse, Pierre Bonnard, Pablo Picasso, and Georges Braque introduced new shapes, influences, colors, and patterns into the aesthetic vocabulary. The Ballets Russes inspired an infusion of exotic colors, fabrics, and harem styles. Increasingly, the old order was ushered out and a new more individualistic world entered; New York was on the verge of becoming an international financial center; Americans were looking outward, ever more curious and cosmopolitan. For someone with a talent to tweak convention and draw deftly from classical and contemporary culture alike, it was an auspicious moment.

Drawing on the talents of Vaslav Nijinsky, Pablo Picasso, Coco Chanel, Igor Stravinsky, George Balanchine, Erik Satie, Richard Strauss, Henri Matisse, and André Derain, among others, Sergei Diaghilev's Ballets Russes daringly synthesized choreography, music, visual art, and bravado performance and exemplified the avant-garde creativity cropping up in Europe.

CHAPTER TWO

THE TRAINING OF A CONNOISSEUR

1920-1923

he New York School of Fine and Applied Art circa 1920 had a hint of snobbery attached to it, for founder Frank Alvah Parsons intended to cultivate only professionals who would win the most prominent commissions and move easily among the influential. Alumnae like Eleanor Brown of McMillen Inc., with her cool architectural style, and Elsie Cobb Wilson, trailing embassies and Blisses in her wake, personified Parsons' ideal. To breed similar successes, Parsons staffed his school with the most stylish practitioners of the day, among them Elsie de Wolfe, Ogden Codman Jr., and William Adams Delano of the architectural firm Delano and Aldrich. Then he sought a certain type of candidate— promising and potentially worldly—and insisted on a personal meeting with each applicant to ascertain suitability for his purpose. He was savvy enough to accept a few socialites, for while they might never become serious professionals, they could lend the school a certain cachet, as well as good connections. Given such ambitions, it was unusual to take on a scholarship boy of indifferent background. (And as the introverted teenager from

T astemaker William Odom, first director of the New York School of Fine and Applied Art's Paris Ateliers, championed understated elegance and George Stacey. While Frank Alvah Parsons provided Stacey with his first break, a rare scholarship to the design school, it was Odom, a connoisseur of Italian furniture and Savile Row suits, who granted Stacey the game-changing opportunity to study in Paris. Odom was the first to recognize Stacey's keen eye for French furniture.

Stratford, Connecticut was incapable of glibly charming his way through an interview, Stacey's scholarship was surely awarded solely on the basis of talent.)

Parsons' pedagogic mission was as lofty as his selection process: the school scoffed at the idea of merely equipping professionals with a pack of workaday design tools and instead aimed to train a discerning eye. The archconservative educator Parsons dismissed the Arts and Crafts movement as a passing fancy while worshipping the École des Beaux-Arts, which he emulated at his school. Course work was designed to cultivate connoisseurship above all other skills, centering on life drawing, antiquity, the Renaissance, and eighteenth-century architecture and decorative arts. But slavish imitation of these styles was never the point; historical styles were to be the inspiration for creating relevant contemporary design.

Aesthetics permeated every aspect of the school. It was expected that students would incorporate beauty, elegance, and refinement—qualities far too essential to relegate to a theoretical backwater—into every facet of life and design, which were of course considered inseparable. In adherence to this dictum, design had to be more than a set of plans; it had to integrate successfully into actual, functional lifestyles (*appropriate* was the code word of the day), as well as be smart, simple, and stylish. Personal elegance—the outward manifestation of one's dedication to beauty—was stressed just as much as design fluency; a memo even circulated among school faculty to remind them that "Chic is emphatically necessary." In the same spirit, no detail, however small, was unworthy of the attention of a true aesthete. Students were taught that even the simple placement of drawing tools on a desk was worth consideration in the pursuit of style. Faculty member William Odom, whom the impeccable Eleanor Brown described with awe as a man who "could not place a book on a table that it did not look special," exemplified this philosophy more than any other mortal.

At Parsons' insistence, Odom extended his refinement to the creation of the Paris study program, the Paris Ateliers. While studying in Paris was a natural extension of the French-centric curriculum, the genius of the program was its reinforcement of the school's commitment to firsthand aesthetic experience. Students visited antique dealers on the Quai Voltaire and fine workrooms such as Jansen, traveled to measure architectural details in château country, sketched at Versailles and Fontainebleau, and explored Paris treasures such as the Hôtel de Soubise. Odom himself would encourage students to run their hands over the carving on an eighteenth-century chair, as well as its underside, to gain a tangible understanding of craftsmanship and proportion. And in the course of all the touching, measuring, drawing, visiting, and viewing of exemplars of eighteenth-century excellence, students became intimately knowledgable of French design in a way that no textbook, lecture, or even museum visit could replicate.

Equally important knowledge of other French ways—sophistication, in fact—came from indirect sources. Depending on their areas of specialization, students were admitted into the best houses and private apartments, attended receptions, and viewed couture collections, for Odom had, of course, arranged a stellar list of school patrons that included the Marquise de Ganay, the painter Walter Gay, and Jean Guiffrey, the conservator of the Louvre, to "insure entrance into châteaux and famous private houses not generally accessible to the public." While many of the classes were conducted as

*K*ey *to William Odom's Paris curriculum was the development of personal connoisseurship, fostered by on-site measuring of boiserie at the Petit Trianon, observation in Jansen's workroom, visits to Parisian antique dealers, and drawing tours to Malmaison, Compiègne, Fontainebleau, and the Loire Valley. Among the elegant students lined up in front of the school before embarking on a sightseeing tour, Stacey stands third from the left in the second row (he can be identified by his receding hairline).*

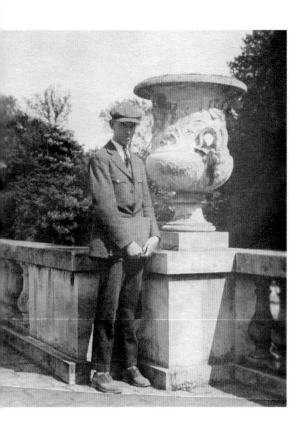

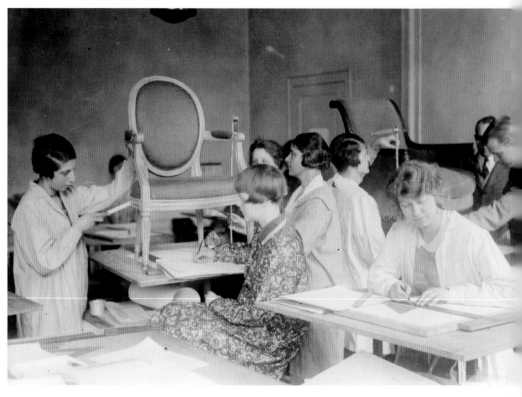

With sketchbook in hand and slightly short trousers, the young Stacey pauses during a drawing outing (above, left). He had been sketching houses since his youth, but design school attuned his eye to classical architecture and proportion. As personal chic was "emphatically necessary" at Parsons' school, one hopes Stacey's dusty shoes can be attributed to strolling on garden paths rather than negligence.

Precise measuring was considered the key to learning the proper relationships between parts. William Odom required students to measure and draw eighteenth-century furniture (above, right); they also drew works of period architecture. Odom taught his students to place their hands on the undersides of chairs to understand all aspects of craftsmanship, as well as the thickness of the wood used. Stacey would apply these lessons outside the classroom in his obsessive quest for antiques.

"promenade lectures," any actual classroom work took place at the aristocratic school headquarters in the Hôtel de Chaulnes on the Place des Vosges (now the elegant home of the three-star restaurant l'Ambroisie), where it was intended that students would absorb the lessons of perfect scale and detail via sheer proximity to the ideal.

Stacey spent his first three years at the New York School of Fine and Applied Art, then located on the Upper West Side, immersed in rigorous mandatory coursework. It was a superb platform for the disciplined development of talent. The first year was devoted to the foundations of design—structure, color, and freehand and mechanical drawing; the second year continued the study of design foundations while adding courses in lighting and the all-important introduction to historical styles, which would be the focus of the third year. The optional fourth year was designated for postgraduate specialization. All years emphasized museum visits, sketching, and the general cultivation of the connoisseur's eye. Given the relatively small size of the school, the faculty was readily available to the students, providing the opportunity for close mentoring relationships. Within this nurturing environment, Stacey developed a close bond with an instructor, one whom friends recounted he would visit loyally for the rest of her life.

If Stacey hadn't caught the eye of another instructor, William Odom, circumstances never would have allowed him the experience of the Paris Ateliers, yet another expense beyond the means of Alford Stacey, who shows up in the 1920 U.S. Census as a humble "lumberman at a sawmill." But Odom, suspecting talent, devised a test to ascertain Stacey's worthiness of a Paris scholarship. Under the pretext of having Stacey deliver some papers to his New York apartment (actually a luxury hotel suite, where the ever-discriminating Odom had painted the walls, slipcovered the hotel furniture in off-white damask, and even supplemented the decor with his own antiques and many flowers), Odom asked Stacey to identify the piece of furniture he liked best. Three years of historical study, museum sketching, haunting antique stores, and exposure via the New York School of Fine and Applied Art had worked its Pygmalion effect on the lumberman's son: Stacey's appraising eye quickly selected the finest antique in the room, demonstrating

The student lounge of the Paris Ateliers on the historic Place des Vosges. Odom had relocated the school to the Hôtel de Chaulnes (now the location of the magnificent l'Ambroisie restaurant) believing that hours spent in superb architecture would transmit invaluable lessons of proportion and design to his students. Stanley Barrows, a later director of Parsons, also considered experiencing fine architecture fundamental to an interior designer's training. The approach succeeded with Stacey, who would later be known for his sense of proportion and placement.

precocious connoisseurship and a keen eye for detail that prompted Odom to arrange a Parisian scholarship for Stacey. According to legend, Odom was so impressed that he extended a scholarship to the Paris Ateliers right then and there in the hotel suite.

Sailing for France on the *Rochambeau* in 1922 marked a turning point for Stacey. With its glorious urban design, limestone architecture, and illustrious museums, Paris was a *coup de coeur* for the aesthetically passionate young New Englander and would remain so throughout his life. Meanwhile, the Paris Ateliers continued the refinement of Stacey. As in New York, the school emphasized sketching from life, an exercise that Stacey evidently valued, given that he guarded among his possessions a tattered sketching pass to the Musée des Arts Décoratifs, as well as a photo of himself clutching his sketch pad. The outings sharpened his historical understanding, attuned his eye to craftsmanship, and stimulated his intellect.

W hen in New York, Odom lived in luxury hotels such as the Pierre, where his fastidious taste necessitated painting the walls, rearranging and supplementing hotel furniture with his own antiques and slipcovers in off-white damask, and adding flowers. Odom summoned Stacey to such a room and asked him to point out the best antique prior to awarding him a scholarship to Paris.

Best of all, Paris was the center for the French furniture that already enticed him. While the school set up private visits to many of the finest dealers in town, Stacey devised his own supplementary antique study program. Designer Ethel Smith, who would later distinguish herself with a fifty-year career at McMillen, wryly recalled how she and Stacey would compete every day in Paris to find the most interesting antique. Invariably, the antique-obsessed Stacey won, never ceasing the hunt until he was certain he had triumphed. While the predictable result of the prescribed school program was that Stacey became a devotee of classicism, symmetry, and the eighteenth century, its unintended side effect was a lifelong compulsion to antique and acquire.

Odom's influence on Stacey extended well beyond the scholarship to Paris. The cool, controlled signatures of Odom's style echo strikingly in Stacey's work through-

out his career. The love of symmetry, subdued wall color with stronger colors in the foreground, the mixing of small-scaled custom-upholstered chairs dimensioned to complement eighteenth-century antiques, the beautifully balanced wall arrangements, the disciplined restraint and love of the neoclassical are all elements of Odom's work which infiltrated the Stacey oeuvre. Like Stacey, Odom loved objects as much as furniture—his exquisite collection of opaline glass glows to this day in a cabinet at the Musée des Arts Décoratifs in Paris—and was drawn to rich fabrics to contrast with the simplicity of the backgrounds he created.

Odom's insistence that classes be held in the elegant Hôtel de Chaulnes on the Place des Vosges was not lost on Stacey, either: the lessons of placement and proportion gained from intimate knowledge of these rooms were continually exhibited in Stacey's own rooms. Stacey could take a vast room in a palace or a great room in the country and impose a serene order on the space through thoughtful scale and furniture placement. Succeeding generations of designers would in turn admire the seamless spatial accord of furniture distribution, art arrangement, and positioning of objects on surfaces (Albert Hadley saved published photos of Stacey rooms in his personal design notebooks) and carry the tradition forward.

Perhaps it was a glimpse of self-recognition that made Odom an aspirational figure for Stacey. Beyond the nascent connoisseurship, there were other similarities. Both men came from backgrounds indifferent to their artistry and sublimated their insecurity in the pursuit of beauty. The diffidence displayed by both men (Odom was known at times to communicate to his students indirectly through others, as it was too painful for him to address them directly)—and Odom's unlikely but evident success—were also likely encouraging for the shy Stacey. The reputedly sumptuous lifestyle of William Odom—summers in Venice at the Palazzo Barbaro, a Rolls-Royce with perfectly liveried driver that crossed the Atlantic with Odom twice a year, two hundred bespoke Huntsman suits, and a valet—was footed by the profits of the antique business he operated in parallel with his responsibilities at the school. Plausibly, Stacey's own venture as an antique dealer in Paris was inspired by Odom's example.

The training at the New York School of Fine and Applied Art, in particular the Paris period, was a touchstone throughout Stacey's career. His fine eye for

*S*tacey retained his heavily used student drawing pass to the *Musée des Arts Décoratifs (above) as a happy memento of his student days in Paris. When he wasn't pursuing his studies or drawing, he vied with Ethel Smith in a daily competition to seek out the best antique. Smith, a future pillar of the interior design firm McMillen, would recall that Stacey always won.*

The similarity of William Odom's taste and George Stacey's taste is striking: the careful symmetry, monochromatic walls, floor, and upholstery, balanced wall compositions, late eighteenth-century French furniture, neoclassical objects, and pairs seen in the William Odom exhibition at McMillen (opposite) translated seamlessly into Stacey interiors, as can be seen by comparing this photo to the photo of Stacey's own apartment on page 114.

antiques gained him his ten successful years as a dealer and became the basis of his reputation for knowledge of French furniture. The discriminating style of Odom, although never completely assimilated by the somewhat bohemian Stacey, added polish to the small-town boy. That polish, combined with the urbane veneer bestowed by a few years in Paris and a quick wit, endowed Stacey with entrée to—and staying power in—the realm of the sophisticated glamorous women who would become the heart of his business.

From a larger perspective, the emphasis on classical design as the departure point for contemporary design provided Stacey's eclectic and dynamic practice with a stabilizing foundation. While Stacey's rooms never looked the same, as they were invariably responsive to the characters of his clients and the spirit of the time, they always displayed the poise and grace gleaned from his classical training. As Stacey nimbly created design responses from one era to the next and wandered onto new aesthetic terrain with Asian furniture or a pared-down postwar sensibility, he brought to each project perfect pitch for quality and balance, whatever the idiom.

The social environment of design school, as well as its training, provided much-needed oxygen for the tentative Stacey. As his talents began to develop and a vision of a professional future came into focus, Stacey's confidence grew. For the first time, friends appear on record. In addition to rapport with faculty members and the friendly competition with Ethel Smith, Stacey began a lifetime pattern of associating with others on parallel artistic paths; the thoughts, careers, experiments, and inclinations of these fellow artists would stimulate his own artistic process, opening his work to new influences and ideas.

One such friend was Daniel Cooper, a soft-spoken modernist who served as witness for George's passport application and received George's mail (Cooper lived near the school), including the treasured passport. With classicism as a common design vocabulary, the two friends could appreciate each other's vision while pursuing divergent design paths. After graduation, while Stacey swanned with the smart set and trawled for eighteenth-century furniture, Cooper designed the penthouse of the Museum of Modern Art, as well as the interiors for the Long Island house Edward Durell Stone designed for Museum of Modern Art president Conger Goodyear, authored a design book advocating artist-craftsmen such as Dorothy Liebes, the prominent textile designer, and founded the American Institute of Interior Designers.

Design school changed Stacey, providing him with the skills and confidence to experiment and mature as a designer. Perhaps the only blight on the design school years was a Parisian visit from his mother—surely an encumbrance to any child who is just spreading his wings and does so best without the inhibiting observation of a parent. At the same time, Stacey's physical traits converged into the combination of lanky frame, retroussé nose, fair complexion, and receding hairline that would characterize him for the rest of his life. This passport portrait, coupled with the propensities exhibited at the New York School of Fine and Applied Art, convey a strong indication of the man George Stacey was to become.

CHAPTER THREE

A FRANCOPHILE IN THE JAZZ AGE

1923–1933

The collective appeal of *cocktails américains* in Montparnasse (it was Prohibition after all in the United States, and Stacey liked a good drink), a favorable exchange rate, and an avant-garde culture that nurtured Josephine Baker, Coco Chanel, and Pablo Picasso drew Stacey back to Paris after graduation.

Stacey's first professional venture was a clever extension of his favorite pastime: the pursuit and acquisition of antiques, which he exported to the United States for sale. While a 1928 *House & Garden* story also describes Stacey as a decorator in Paris, it was the antique end of the business that flourished, for its timing was superb. America in the 1920s was flush and, encouraged by a developing consumer economy, in the mood to acquire. Advertisements touted appliances, furniture, and home accessories to housewives, fostering a cult of domesticity that anchored the economy. (All these goods were meant, of course, to transform the quality of life.) For the well-heeled sophisticate who rarely entered the kitchen, the impulse to acquire translated—once again—into purchasing objects to reflect

culture, interests, and social position. Antiques from France were objects of desire.

The business partnership that Stacey established was as brilliant as the timing. While Stacey at first worked independently—ship manifests show him making several Atlantic crossings, presumably to market his wares—fate intervened in the guise of Hans van Nes. In 1926, Stacey met van Nes, who was lingering in Paris after earning a degree at the Sorbonne; shortly afterward, the two combined forces in the antiques venture. Descended from the seventeenth-century Dutch naval hero Hans van Nes, whose portrait hangs in the Rijksmuseum, young van Nes was the son of a prosperous Midwestern grain merchant and a Francophile mother who had brought her son along on her extended stays in France. Like Stacey, van Nes knew his way around France, spoke French, and was artistic—he could draw beautifully and had a keen eye for form and light that he later put to good use as a professional photographer—but his most significant contribution to the partnership was charm. (A testament to his appeal is his wife's account of their initial meeting: she, a professional pianist, arrived at his photography studio for publicity shots, only to be greeted by a sleepy van Nes wearing a silk dressing gown—his charisma was such that despite the dubious start, she had dinner with him the next evening and married him shortly thereafter.)

Van Nes and Stacey were perfect complements. Stacey, the introvert with the Odom-trained eye, focused on purchasing in France. By now a confirmed antique hunter, he haunted the obscure estate sales, flea markets, country auctions, and docks that yielded the best finds at the most favorable prices. Van Nes, confident and debonair, oversaw sales in New York. He intuitively understood that antiques conveyed romance, history, culture, and status, which made light work of moving inventory in the optimistic 1920s. Unlike Odom, who sold privately to selected decorators like Elsie Cobb Wilson and Eleanor Brown, Stacey and van Nes opened a store at 576 Madison Avenue. With van Nes in New York, sales mounted (the partnership had—despite Black Tuesday—a banner year in 1929), and the two men enjoyed their first press attention, including a photo in *Vogue*, and established a reputation for style. Judging from remaining photos, it seems they specialized in furniture with bold neoclassical lines. Quite useful for future endeavors, too, was a storefront presence and a

C haracteristic, intuitive, and artistic, Hans van Nes was the ideal partner for Stacey's growing antiques business. While the reserved Stacey scouted for antiques in France, the genial van Nes deftly closed sales in their Madison Avenue store. Later, van Nes taught Stacey how the camera lens captures space and photographed Stacey's projects for publication in Town & Country and House & Garden. An avid sailor whose nautical adventures with his children became the subject of a movie, van Nes is seen leaning against a mast in Saint-Raphaël in the south of France.

modicum of publicity that lent Stacey's name its first faint ring of recognition in New York.

Other enduring friendships also formed in Paris. Andrew Heiskell, the journalist and future chairman of Time Inc., happened to be studying in Paris at the time, and as late as the 1990s, the two would meet to reminisce over drinks. Stacey also met the New York–born painter Helen Marshall, who would become his soul mate, muse, and romantic ideal. Photos of a jaunty twosome testify to a fondly remembered vacation in Cassis and the leavening effect Marshall had on Stacey. Like van Nes, Marshall had an effervescent personality that complemented the darker temperament of Stacey, but

D*ue to his stylish eye, Stacey began to attract notice as an antique dealer. In 1932,* Vogue *featured an Empire table from Stacey's store. While the tailored lines of the table echo the inherent understatement in Stacey's designs, the orb lamp and Moroccan rug align with his penchant for contrast and innovation. As Frederick P. Victoria became a longtime friend and collaborator, it is prophetic that Victoria's Regency chair (left) complements the Stacey table.*

As a young Parisian antique dealer, Stacey's apartment was published in House & Garden in 1928. His sitting room already reveals the hallmarks of his style: the glamour of gilt wood, crystal drops, and mirror contrasting with neoclassical elements, such as the bust on the mantel, Empire candlestick, and Louis XVI chair. The authoritative wall compositions mixing paintings, sconces, and bibelots, and the serenity of pairs would also become a Stacey signature.

T hough Stacey embraced much of the Odom doctrine, his own style was less studied,
more offhand. Stacey's Parisian bedroom exhibited his lifelong affinity for objects
but retained its composure through the repeated use of pairs—in this case, girandoles,
urn lamps, urn vases, and wall-mounted terme oil lamps—and disciplined neoclassical
furniture; in contrast, ashes nonchalantly spill over the hearth. Blithely hanging pictures
on doors also was consistent with Stacey's confidently relaxed approach to classic design.

L ifelong friend Helen Sieglin Marshall, the daughter of a New York wine importer, and an accomplished and exhibited painter in London and New York, would always command Stacey's special affection. A photo snapped during a magical summer in Cassis–of which Stacey always spoke fondly–testifies to the leavening effect of Marshall's sparkling personality on the hesitant and insecure Stacey. Her subsequent marriage to an elegant Englishman would devastate Stacey.

beyond the superficial differences, the two shared an uncanny closeness. Even when the two were working on opposite sides of the Atlantic, the themes Marshall would explore on canvas mirrored themes Stacey explored in interior design. Close friends say Stacey spoke of Marshall frequently throughout his life.

The photos of Stacey's Paris apartment in a 1928 *House & Garden* story titled "A Little Portfolio of French Interiors" ("shown as a contrast to modernist rooms," the writer explained) already contain the eighteenth-century leitmotifs which distinguish the Stacey style throughout his career: painted Louis XVI chairs, neo-classical busts, candelabra with rock crystal drops, urns, opaline glass, bouillotte lamps, and poised wall arrange-ments combining art, sconces, and brackets. While cool neoclassicism, the preference of Odom, predominates, Stacey also exerts his own more fluid and whimsical taste into the rooms with sparkling girandoles, a grace-fully curved provincial Louis XV writing table, and tôle flowers. Possibly the fastidious William Odom would not have approved of the previous night's ashes spilling from the mantel box onto the hearth. Whether the ashes were negligent oversight or an artful decision, the detail is revealing: Stacey's rooms, even the most grand, had a casual attitude. Though acclaimed for exquisiteness, he embraced imperfection–informal elements, objets trouvés, and insouciant disregard for convention would forever appear in his work.

The 1925 Exposition Internationale des Arts Décoratifs et Industriels Modernes unveiled another novelty from Paris–design influenced by industrial machinery and materials–which Stacey would observe. Despite a positive public response to the mostly metal-and-glass furniture with geometric lines, design editor Richardson Wright slammed the new furniture as "ele-phantine and out of proportion" (justifying Odom's lip-curled indifference to the new aesthetic). Slightly later, in the sensitive hands of Jean-Michel Frank, refined shagreen, ivory, parchment, and split-straw marquetry furniture with pared-down lines proved modernism's capacity for elegance, a capability Stacey noted and filed.

Stacey observed the modernist trends in Paris from a singular vantage point. While his apartment reflected his love of the eighteenth century as well as his business venture in antiques (it is quite possible that Stacey, like many *antiquaires*, considered all possessions potential inventory and his home served as a glorified warehouse), his friendships with the modernist Daniel Cooper, painter Helen Marshall, and van Nes (then in his early stages of flirtation with photography) and their friends made him aware of the aesthetic dialogues of the day. Not only did Stacey observe the new currents, but some of them would find expression shortly in his own work. His interest in new genres, fostered by his training at design school, would continually renew his aesthetic as a designer.

In the United States, however, style setters were just as likely to furnish their houses with eighteenth-century furniture as experiment with mirror and mica. For the smart set, the trend was definitely conservative. *House & Garden* published J. H. Carstairs' Georgian house designed by John Russell Pope, which Mrs. Carstairs, following time-honored British tradition, filled with French furniture. Eleanor Brown of McMillen, always Odom's most avid client, created her stylish signature Directoire rooms, while Diane Tate and Marian Hall purveyed well-bred English taste to those who could afford their services. Elsie de Wolfe continued with her doctrine of neoclassical suitability, venturing into a somewhat darkened palette. While good taste abounded, no one had yet arrived on the scene to make a convincing case for experimentation.

After the crash in 1929, it was not clear how seriously the economy was wounded or how lives would be affected on a practical basis. While wary, the clientele for antiques continued to purchase, and Stacey maintained the antique business for several more years, even after van Nes left the partnership in 1930 and terminated the lease on the store. (Although the antique business folded and their lives assumed different miens—van Nes became a successful commercial photographer, avid sailor, and father of six—the two men stayed in contact. When Hans van Nes Jr. was stationed in France in the 1950s, he was sent off with Stacey's château address in his kit.) As the Depression dragged on, and after the death of Alford Stacey in 1933, Stacey wended his way back to New York. By then, he was a man somewhat different from the boy who had first gone to Paris in 1922. Paris had become a second home and would be so for the rest of his life, a place to which he retreated not so much to work as to replenish his psyche and creativity. He had also attained renown for his eye for French furniture, an international perspective, and the confidence of having met with success. Most significantly, the culture of ideas, discourse, and aesthetics had invested his eye with worldliness.

A tidy and relaxed Stacey on the beach reveals his emerging self-confidence and style. The pairing of a tie with sporty knickerbockers mirrors the classic/casual duality in Stacey's designs.

CHAPTER FOUR

A CHIC HOUSE FOR AN "IT GIRL"

1933–1935

Crossing the Atlantic in 1933 gave Stacey more than a week to ponder his next step. Essentially an independent spirit, he determined that if he had to work for someone else, it could only be for one decorator: Rose Cumming. Cumming's instinct for theater, glamour, and fantasy were unrivaled. Her work exuded a sensuous negligence and reveled in color—in one dining room, she left an exposed electrical box above the dining table, painted the ceiling deep turquoise, scattered the table with random nautilus shells, and extemporized a planter from what appears to be a gilt-wood sleigh.

It is clear how Rose Cumming's lush romanticism would have appealed to Stacey as the corollary to the disciplined chic of Odom. Cumming, often ill-kempt and highly emotional, was quite the opposite of Odom, whose taste was arguably too glacially perfect. Cumming's work represented the counterbalance to Stacey's temperament: the searching bohemian free spirit, intuitive colorist, and incurable collector. Like Stacey, Cumming went everywhere in her all-consuming pursuit of beauty, including the streets

Stacey returned from Paris to a New York enthralled with innovation and machine-age elegance. Just as the 1930 Chrysler Building (above) handily translated the French art deco style for America, Stacey translated the ideas he had encountered during his formative years in Paris into an American design idiom.

For this moody portrait (opposite), Hans van Nes surrounded Stacey with elements that defined his style in the 1930s—a neoclassical urn, sfumato lines, and dramatic scale. The yin-yang profiles of Stacey and the urn made a virtue of his prominent forehead.

of New York, where rendering artist Jeremiah Goodman remembers Miss Cumming "like a bag lady, ferreting through items left on the sidewalk for the trash collector." She had a mystical communion with her objects and was known to renege on a sale when she found herself unable to part with a favorite piece. Satin and rich, seductive fabrics, as well as exquisite English chintzes, were Cumming's trademark materials. Her use of pure, brilliant, clear color was virtuosic. Jade, blue, lilac, cyclamen, brilliant yellows, bronzes—exuberant colors not figuring in either the new moderne rooms or the controlled, tasteful settings of the McMillens, Tate and Halls, and Elsie de Wolfes of the day—dominated the Rose Cumming world.

This fascinating eccentric was rumored to be the mistress of financier and Metropolitan Opera benefactor Otto Kahn. Whether true or not, with her caprices, gauzy dresses, and penchant for sipping bourbon from a teacup, Rose Cumming was both exotic and forbidding. Stacey experienced trepidation as he walked to his interview. "No one who has seen or talked to Miss Cumming could manage by any trick of the imagination to think of her as the girl next door," he recalled dryly, "and by the time I actually arrived in her presence, I needed a drink to bolster my rapidly collapsing ego." Fortunately, he managed to pull his thirty-two-year-old self together, marshaled his considerable experience and credentials, and got the desired job. The hitch was that it was the Depression (and presumably one took anything that came one's way), so Stacey became Miss Cumming's humble jack-of-all-trades. Perhaps Cumming didn't have a lot of work at that time—a situation that would certainly not have posed a problem if Otto Kahn were underwriting the business—for Stacey found himself sweeping the cellar rather too often.

As an accomplished raconteur who knew the power of exaggeration, Stacey would have us believe his employment with Rose Cumming lasted exactly one day before he handed back his broom. The actual sequence of events lasted somewhat longer, at least a matter of weeks, if not months. One prophetic day shortly after Stacey had begun working for Cumming, young Mrs. Ward Cheney, daughter of Henry P. Davison, Wall Street wunderkind and keystone of the J. P. Morgan empire, sailed into the Madison Avenue store, bringing in her wake repercussions that would fundamentally shape Stacey's career.

U pon returning to America after ten years in Paris, Stacey vowed to work only for Rose Cumming (above), whose lush romanticism counterbalanced the disciplined chic of Odom. Though Miss Cumming and Stacey were kindred bohemian spirits and incurable collectors, Stacey approached the exotic decorator with trepidation: "No one who has seen or talked to Miss Cumming could manage by any trick of the imagination to think of her as the girl next door," he dryly recalled.

Both were intuitive colorists: Cumming's use of pure, brilliant color was virtuosic, and ultimately Stacey would be renowned for his jewel-toned palette. Like Stacey, Cumming went everywhere in her pursuit of beautiful objects. Rendering artist Jeremiah Goodman remembers Cumming "like a bag lady, ferreting through items left on the sidewalk for the trash collector." Cumming unleased her all-out magic on her own living room (opposite).

By contemporary accounts, Frances Cheney was the It Girl of the moment, a daring, stylish iconoclast. Her young husband, Ward Cheney, heir to the Cheney silk empire, Yale varsity oarsman, translator of Aeschylus, art aficionado, and friend of Gerald Murphy, was her elegant counterpart. They had been introduced by their respective best friends, Marie and Sonny Whitney (Marie later became Mrs. Averell Harriman, at which point she became a Stacey client as well), and were married mere weeks later (impulsiveness being a pronounced trait in Frances Cheney) in a wedding that the press heralded as the wedding of the season. Ward donned a top hat and carried a jaunty cane; Frances wore a fashionably short white dress trailing yards of train, tulle, and white fox. The unconventional Frances brought her widowed mother along on the honeymoon, and the ever-accommodating Ward fell into step with the unusual arrangement. As with many things related to the couple, their honeymoon apartment at 4 East 66th Street attracted media attention: decorated by Elsie Cobb Wilson, right down to its back-painted mirrors, chinoiserie screens, and lace-trimmed lampshades, it landed on the pages of *Town & Country*.

By nature, Frances Cheney gravitated to new ideas, adventure, and experimentation. Amidst a world of sober Republicans, she espoused liberal Democratic views. While the most fashionable New York babies were born at Miss Lippincott's Sanitarium at 667 Madison Avenue, with champagne and meals sent up from the Colony Restaurant below, Frankie, as she was known, opted for progressive home births. (She even delivered one daughter on her Fifth Avenue kitchen table.) Nor were elegant pedigrees Frankie's thing; *she* chose to stroll Manhattan with an unleashed, retired seeing-eye dog. And finally, there was her adventurous personal style—manifested daily in striking clothes calculated to set her apart from the debutante pack *and* attract notice. Soon her interiors would follow suit.

Others were also beginning to share Frankie's curiosity and restlessness amidst the status quo. Bored with traditional society, a world of established families, and prescribed destinations, Frances' friend Sonny Whitney and his cousin Jock Whitney began to mix among a group culled from the worlds of finance, media, publishing, theater, Hollywood, and the arts. The phenomenon, later known as Café Society, represented a fluid crossing of boundaries. Frankie, operating her

Employment with Cumming proved providential to Stacey's career, as well as to his aesthetic development: while sweeping Cumming's cellar, Stacey met the young and very rich Frances Davison Cheney. For Frances' wedding, heralded by the press as the wedding of the season, Ward Cheney (above) arrived elegantly turned out in spats, top hat, and cane, while the bride wore dashing head-to-toe white fox and trailed yards of tulle. Though the glamorous newlyweds hired Elsie Cobb Wilson to decorate their honeymoon apartment on Fifth Avenue, Frances Cheney would later seek more adventurous interiors with George Stacey.

In 1934, Frances Cheney and her sister posed for Cecil Beaton and Vogue in a Stacey-designed living room (opposite).

At first, the young Cheneys intended to build a proper Georgian house on the Davison family property at Peacock Point. However, as Frances had an inclination for high style, a conservative house similar to her mother's was not to be. Although drawings for Frances and Ward Cheney's house were well advanced when the pair went for a visit to Monticello (below, left), upon arriving, Frankie rushed a call to her architect to stop the project. Thomas Jefferson had provided her with a new inspiration: an art deco octagonal house.

For the Cheneys' modernist Monticello (below, right), Stacey created a living room worthy of a contemporary Jefferson that blended glamour, historicism, and swagger with stylish restraint (opposite). Striking in its simplicity and integating classical and modern styles, the room revealed Stacey's training by Frank Alvah Parsons, who vaunted the study of historical space as the foundation for relevant contemporary design. The wood swags flanking the fireplace were the first of many commissions Stacey placed with Frederick P. Victoria throughout his career.

own art gallery, lobbying for U.S. intervention in World War II (she even set up an office, where she was photographed by *Harper's Bazaar*'s Louise Dahl-Wolfe), ordering couture clothes, and dripping jewelry, embodied every aspect of Café Society. (Ever the It Girl, Frankie could always draw the oxygen out of a room. English designer Nicky Haslam remembers the power of the sixty-year-old Frankie in her impeccable Parisian clothes, so magnetic a presence that even his practiced eye could not register any design details in the room, so taken was he with her charm.)

Upon their marriage, a piece of land on Peacock Point, the family property in Locust Valley, New York, was designated for a country house for Frankie and Ward. At first, the young Cheneys intended to build a proper Georgian house in keeping with the main house at Peacock Point. But given Frankie's inclination to high style, a conservative house like her mother's was not to be. Although the drawings for the house were well advanced when Frankie and Ward Cheney went off for a visit to Monticello, after arriving at their destination, Frankie rushed a call to her architect to stop the project. Thomas Jefferson had inspired a new vision: an art deco octagonal house. Characteristically—and fortunately—the Cheneys had hired a progressive young architect, Harvey Stevenson, who proved an adept stylist. Stevenson easily transitioned from Georgian house to art deco pavillon of cinder block (at the time

S teuben and English crystal
smartly offset classically
inspired klismos chairs, plaster
medallions, rosettes, consoles, urns,
and pedestals in the chic living
room Stacey designed for Ward
and Frances Cheney. Sleek satin
upholstery groupings promote
conviviality, while the dynamic
interplay of light and dark tones
adds panache to a poised room.

an innovative building material, today bemoaned by its current owner for its porosity). In fact, Stevenson was so proficient in moderne architectural vocabulary that by the end of the 1930s, he had designed New York City's East River Drive with its deco dolphin-sculpted entrance, as well as the New York City World's Fair Administration Building.

Once the architecture for Frankie's house was on track, she turned her attention to the interiors. It was natural for Frankie to look to the *outré* talent of Rose Cumming. It was also natural for the impulsive, confident Mrs. Cheney not to bother with an appointment and to sweep unannounced into the store. This evidently wasn't the right way to approach Rose Cumming, for the meeting began inauspiciously and deteriorated by the moment. Cumming sized up her visitor as too young and too inexperienced to have much style or to be of any interest (little did she know) and airily passed Frankie off to her assistant. Summoning George Stacey (Frankie would later recall that he came up from the basement with a broom in hand) turned out to be the perfect answer. With an ability to weave broad design influences into a polished cosmopolitan whole, Stacey brought the design equivalent of Café Society to the new Cheney house.

With little other than sweeping cellars to distract him, Stacey threw himself into the Cheney project. That very evening, he drew preliminary sketches for review the next day with the new client. Conjuring the signature sculptures at Les Deux Magots in Paris, he added a small mandarin figure by the fireplace on a whim; this nonsensical detail, so aligned with her own sensibility, captivated Frankie, laying a foundation for what would become a seven-project design partnership and lifelong friendship. But despite the promising start, Cheney and Stacey had one obstacle to clear. While there is no available backstory of the parting of Rose Cumming and George Stacey, we do know Stacey telephoned Frances Cheney somewhat later to explain that he could no longer work on her house, as he was no longer employed by Miss Cumming. Mrs. Cheney simply didn't recognize this as an impediment—very few things were to her—and followed Stacey to his next short-lived engagement, this one at a firm named Taylor and Low. Fortunately for Stacey, who worked best alone, the momentum of the Cheney job soon allowed him to establish his own office.

S tacey's bedrooms spoke of worldly luxury. In the sitting area of the Cheney master suite, white curtains and antique satin slipper chairs, accompanied by sconces and torchères lavished with crystal, frame a window overlooking Long Island Sound. While the high-contrast blue and white scheme lends nautical snappiness, the mix of Regency chandelier, overscaled passementerie, and antiqued mirror table injects both wit and connoisseurship.

Stacey's eye, abetted by Frankie Cheney's confidence, spurred the project to great design heights. While an adventurer in matters of taste, Frances Cheney shared one trait with Americans of previous generations: she wanted only the best, was accustomed to having it, and spared no expense. Needless to say, this helped with the success of the design, and it also contributed a note of comedy. Without hesitation, Cheney and Stacey contacted Steuben to commission a crystal bath tub in the shape of a swan. They were surprised to be politely rebuffed and informed that the company could not attend to such a fabulous request as it was "a little busy" with a challenging commission—the groundbreaking telescope mirrors for the Palomar Observatory in California. Nevertheless, Steuben was able to execute Stacey's design for a crystal bed worthy of a maharaja and a bathroom of antiqued mirror—walls, bathtub, door casings, and moldings, all custom-made.

The resulting house was splendid: a flattened, stylized art deco facade, situated with breathtaking views of Long Island Sound and detailed with spare elegance. The central block contained an octagonal living room with master bedroom and dressing rooms above. Flanking wings accommodated a library, children's and guest rooms, a kitchen, and service quarters. Meals were taken outside overlooking the water; in chilly weather, a table was set up by the fireplace in the living room.

The master suite departed from the clean neoclassicism of the living room to incorporate neobaroque elements against navy blue walls: a high-style door and pediment, a gray lacquered floor with scrolled border of antique white with shrimp pink highlights, a mirrored bed with Steuben ruff (seen reflected in the mirror), and sybaritic fur rugs. The eclectic side chair paid homage to Mies van der Rohe's 1927 Bauhaus lounge chair with its tubular upholstery, while its saber legs reflected the prevailing vogue for the Regency style. Too busy to execute the crystal swan bathtub envisioned by Stacey and Frances Cheney, Steuben placated the duo with the headboard and mirrored architectural trim for her bath.

Albert Hadley noted, "Stacey went over the top and always stayed in the mood of the moment. His work was all very glamorous, just the way it should be." However, Stacey counterbalanced over-the-top glamour with disciplined symmetry: here, a silvered cabinet, mirror, and Regency chair are matched by an identical vignette on the other side of the door. A fantastical mantel of mirrored volutes, towering candelabra, and squared-off seating (reflecting the influence of industrial design), all softened by the voluptuous combination of tufting and ostrich fringe, add cutting-edge sizzle.

Since his return to the United States, Stacey's eye had acquired a handy new facility due to his friendship with Hans van Nes. Using van Nes' expertise as a professional photographer to full advantage, Stacey learned how a camera lens reads space. Van Nes, as a photographer, was keenly aware of light. (His son still recalls his father's mantra: "Light is everything. Light is what you see. Light is *all* you see.") Correspondingly, Stacey's design work reflects the van Nes tutelage, displaying an understanding of how light models a profile, a sensitivity to contrasts of light and dark, a subtle responsiveness to sparkle and nuance, and an awareness of the power of a silhouette, all qualities that make rooms photogenic as well as beautiful. Friendship with a photographer also yielded further pragmatic benefits: van Nes, Stacey's first photographer, had an intimate understanding of Stacey's design perceptions. Over the next decade, a sort of symmetry developed between the two: Stacey would intuitively conceive rooms that would charm a camera, and van Nes would skillfully capture some of Stacey's best work, which ultimately would appear in influential publications.

The Cheneys moved into the house in 1934, and shortly thereafter, the interiors were finished. The house was published to acclaim in *Vogue*, *House & Garden*, and *Town & Country* (twice) and photographed by Cecil Beaton. Like all of Stacey's great work, the Cheney house (also referred to in this book as the Octagon House), captured the spirit of the moment, fusing Ward and Frankie's stylish élan and Stacey's sense of drama and silhouette into a cool, sexy, and surprising monument to an alluring couple.

Vogue described the living room as a "beautiful baroque drawing room, hung with chartreuse-yellow taffeta curtains and with pale chocolate-colored walls." In Stacey's hand, the brilliant hues of Rose Cumming had metamorphosed into a subtle, rich palette. He combined disparate elements with offhand ease: Venetian mirrors and painted furniture, an Anglo-Indian chandelier with art deco neoclassicism, modern upholstery with klismos chairs, eighteenth-century andirons, and modish contemporary rugs. The upholstery was rich ivory satin.

The master suite, which included Frances' mirrored bath and a dressing room for Ward, romantically occupied the entire second floor, with an airy bedroom overlooking Long Island Sound. The bedroom was as glamorous as the living room, evoking, in the words of

*B*oth Frank Lloyd Wright's romantic Fallingwater and the Cheneys' modernist Monticello were designed in the mid-1930s. Whereas Wright displayed strong architectural consistency, Harvey Stevenson, the Cheneys' architect, zigzagged between traditional and modern and residential and industrial architecture. Stevenson shared the Cheneys' and Stacey's spirit of aesthetic adventure, which led him to undertake such diverse projects as the 1930s East River Drive (cited in the AIA Guide to New York City as "a brilliant solution to the intersection of city, river, and highway"), the art deco administration building for the 1939 World's Fair, and an understated modern house for Gary Cooper in Brentwood, California.

Town & Country, a watercolor by Tsuguharu Foujita, with walls colored "a dusky night-bright blue," against which silvery furniture, pale upholstery, crystal, and mirrors sparkled. The delicate floor by the artist Merle Pinkston was painted with sweeping stylized baroque volutes and shells and required special care as well as visual attention: "following the Mohammedan routine," the writer explained, "shoes are removed before entering." The Steuben crystal-rod bed, low-slung chairs with ostrich fringe in the seams, a mirrored rocaille fireplace, a Regency chandelier, eighteenth-century andirons, and a crystal torchère with candles (Albert Hadley noted that tall candles appear consistently in Stacey's work throughout the decades) added subtle and not-so-subtle layers of interest.

In the 1930s, the Cheney house stood out from the crowd by combining glamour with erudition, history with a set designer's instinct, color with quality, designer with client. Other contemporaneous designs also reflected the elegance of the era but from divergent points of view. Fusing man and nature, Frank Lloyd Wright designed the spectacularly romantic Fallingwater for Edgar Kaufmann. Eleanor Brown at McMillen produced her own coolly stylish apartment. In Europe, the Berlin Exposition displayed work by Mies van der Rohe and Walter Gropius. Fashionable Syrie Maugham produced work similar to Stacey's, but her softer emphasis on luxurious upholstered pieces and signature white palette distinguished her rooms from Stacey's color-infused spaces, which exhibited a formalist's acknowledgement of spatial volume, line, light, and profile, as well as an antiquarian's interest in provenance and history.

The house's simplicity and confidence and the dissimilarities of periods, materials, and quality of the furnishings, all balanced by a precise plan and mastery of scale, established a new way to live graciously, one that appealed particularly to the stylish, adventuresome spirit of Frances Cheney's New York friends and became a template for modish sophisticates everywhere. In fact, the house looked as if the celluloid sophisticates Nick and Nora Charles could have lived here. *The Thin Man* and the Cheney house made their debut the same year, a testament to the influence of the camera—Hasselblad or Hollywood genre—on design in the 1930s. For the film, Cedric Gibbons had also translated the bulky, mechanistic look of the 1920s into a more graceful

In London, fashionable Syrie Maugham evoked the same worldly sophistication that Stacey conjured in New York. Maugham's emphasis on luxurious upholstered pieces and her signature white palette distinguished her from Stacey, who embraced color and had an antiquarian's interest in provenance and history and a keen awareness of scale, proportion, and placement.

modernist style. But next to the Cheneys' living room, which referenced diverse cultures and eras and mixed modern materials and old techniques, the Charles' living room looks one-dimensional. For once, real life was more glamorous than film.

Stacey's relationship with Frances Cheney had begun with the silly whimsy of a mandarin figure, acquired momentum during the designing of an iconic house, and deepened into a great friendship. As best friends, Frances and Stacey saw each other nearly every day. Cheney's mother was fond of Stacey's company, also. Stacey joined the competitive croquet games that were fashionable among the Cheneys, Davisons, Harrimans, Guinzburgs, and Swopes of the Long Island set—and those games were the rare instances when Stacey would relinquish his omnipresent cigarette. Holidays were spent with the family, too. Stacey was at Peacock Point so frequently that young nieces and nephews on the compound thought he was family. While Frankie had been the early catalyst for the friendship, Ward Cheney also entered into the equation. In later years, every fall, the Cheneys and Stacey would spend a month in Europe, where Ward and George developed a pattern of slipping off in the morning to antique, gallery hop, and sightsee together. The independent friendships with both husband and wife was a pattern that lasted as long as the Cheneys were alive and one that would repeat itself with future clients.

Despite the increasing recognition of his talent, Stacey's deep insecurity rendered him passive in the realm of self-promotion, his healthy competitive instincts apparent only on the croquet lawn. Many have pointed out that Stacey never spoke about his projects, hesitant to draw attention to something so revealing of himself. With sisterly protectiveness, Frances Cheney and her sister, Alice Gates, promoted Stacey to their friends. (The grateful Stacey cites Frankie's tireless efforts on his behalf in *The Finest Rooms by America's Great Decorators*.) Alice, with a coveted mention on one of the city's best-dressed lists, had as much aesthetic clout as Frances and connections that supplemented her sister's. Through her husband, Artemus Gates—Yale football star, member of the legendary World War I Millionaires' Unit, bank president, and Assistant Secretary of the Navy for Air during the war—Alice knew just about everyone in the ranks of the Establishment that the independent-

minded Frankie eschewed. Buoyed by the glamour of the Octagon House and a critical assist from Alice and Frances, Stacey would soon find himself designing for Harrimans, Harknesses, Mortimers, Whitneys, Vreelands, and Astors, among others.

While Stacey was enjoying his success with the Cheney house, Stacey's good friend from his Paris years, Helen Marshall, had her first success, too—a major exhibit at the Cooling Galleries on New Bond Street in London. *Apollo* magazine wrote what could just as easily have served as a critique of the Cheney house: "Miss Helen Marshall has a strong sense of color used decoratively. She conveys an acute sense of atmosphere.... She interprets with a scientific precision certain articles that hold the spectator's interest, since their appeal to the eye is equally as strong as their appeal to the mind."

Clearly, as artists and friends, Stacey and Marshall, rational classicists dedicated to color, were destined to be soul mates who metaphorically completed each other's sentences. But their relationship had limitations. In 1934, Marshall married advertising man H. Hannath Marshall, an elegant product of English public schools and Oriel College, Oxford, and settled in London. The marriage was crushing for Stacey, who would always regard Helen Marshall as his shining light and perhaps a way to negotiate a life without explicitly defining himself. His military records from the 1940s divulge that the trauma of his friend's marriage devastated him, sending him to a psychiatrist's couch. Fortunately, Alice Gates and Frances Cheney came up with plenty of ways to distract him from his heartbreak. And another fascinating woman, Diana Vreeland, would next take up with Stacey.

MGM designer Cedric Gibbons, shown here at home with his wife, Dolores del Rio, devised high-contrast interiors with stepped recesses and bold geometry specifically to appeal on black-and-white film. Similarly, Stacey's innate sense of profile, scale, and tonal contrast ensured that his work was photogenic in an era of black-and-white photography.

CHAPTER FIVE

LACQUER AND BLACKAMOORS FOR DIANA VREELAND

1935–1942

I n 1935, thirtysomething Mrs. T. Reed Vreeland majestically returned to New York after five years in London, where she had been presented at court and methodically soaked up Paris fashion, assiduously cutting out articles from *Vogue* and *Harper's Bazaar* for her scrapbooks. Not a beauty, she had transformed herself into a striking and memorable presence (and had even acquired a new pronunciation of her name: Dee-AHN-a) among the international set. Reputedly, she and her very handsome husband had run through an inheritance, which in all fairness had perhaps been a casualty of the crash as much as of a lavish London lifestyle, and she now needed to look for work. At the time, *Harper's Bazaar* was on the lookout for an editor who could make news for them in New York as Daisy Fellowes had done for their Paris office. Enter Diana Vreeland—found dancing on the roof of the St. Regis in a white Chanel bolero with red roses in her hair—tastemaker of the twentieth century.

Vreeland was in love with a life that was dazzling and pictorial. If it was larger than life, she discovered it. If it didn't exist, she made it, coaxing from

a New Jersey cobbler a thong sandal based on images from the pornographic museum in Pompeii. Her clothes were high-styled and extreme, even for New York. When she went to Palm Beach, her emerald green shorts with red zippers made news. She had unerring instincts for what was new, distinctive, and destined for importance, discovering Lauren Bacall, publishing the Beatles, and publicizing the bikini as "the most important thing since the atom bomb!" By the late 1930s, she was living at 400 Park Avenue in a striking apartment *not* designed by her friend Elsie de Wolfe. Vreeland was already on to the next big thing, a designer who had recently made a splash with a chic villa on Long Island: George Stacey.

The apartment Stacey designed at 400 Park Avenue suited the bold, well-bred, widely read Vreeland. Like the fashion editor herself, it was supremely confident, limed with exaggeration and embellishment: lacquer, nacre shells, blackamoors, and animal prints. It was also modern, adapting convention to suit new circumstances. Stacey surely fed off Vreeland's energy and confidence—characteristics common to all of Stacey's favorite clients—as well as her prodigious imagination. It was a reciprocated admiration, and Vreeland often tucked tidbits from Stacey into her flamboyant "Why Don't You…" column for *Harper's Bazaar*, a compendium of funny, whimsical, extravagant, and, very occasionally, sensible advice (such as turning one's ermine coat into a bathrobe). The subtext of the column was classic Vreeland: stop being boring and create some interest in your life. And the apartment did just this, rising triumphantly above undistinguished architecture and limited means to exude stylish sophistication.

Stacey and Vreeland spoke the same color language—a daring, brilliant, historic, saturated dialect that few others knew. The Renaissance and its colors were alive and accessible to both. Mark Hampton compared the Stacey palette to that of a Venetian altarpiece, dominated by red and green (like Vreeland's Palm Beach shorts), shimmering elements of yellow and blue, and "over the entire surface, patches of gold for added brilliance and color." For her part, Vreeland obsessed over cinquecento red—"all my life, I've pursued the perfect red…the best red is…the color of a child's cap in *any* Renaissance portrait"—but loved all color. With her fashion-trained eye, she well knew the value of contrast, a cornerstone in Stacey's work, too. "Realize, realize the return of black, and black and

T he visionary editor of Harper's Bazaar, *Carmel Snow, found Diana Vreeland dancing on the roof of the St. Regis in a white Chanel bolero with red roses in her hair. Vreeland was the fashion editor of Snow's dreams: someone who, as Daisy Fellowes had done for the magazine's Paris office, could make news. Soon Vreeland was scribbling worldly advice to readers in her flamboyant "Why Don't You…" column, often offering decorating suggestions based on her design collaboration with George Stacey.*

white, in decoration. It is of tremendous importance," wrote Vreeland to her *Harper's Bazaar* readers.

Other shared affinities also came into play. France, the spiritual home of Stacey and birthplace of Vreeland, created a natural reference point between the two. Improvisation worked for Vreeland, too—it had to, as she needed to toe the line with her budget—so Stacey was able to pack in some ingenious, relaxed surprises, such as using rattan picnic seats as pull-up chairs. Edward Warburg, cofounder of Balanchine's nascent New York City Ballet and also a Stacey client, would remember the Vreelands' apartment as worldly but incongruous with "blackamoors all over the place… and paper-white narcissus in salad bowls." Vreeland, like Stacey, adored objects trailing history and romance, as the controlled clutter of collections in the Vreeland apartment attested. Finally, in the rarified world in which the two existed, they shared an additional subtle bond of understanding—they both worked, loved to work, and *needed* to work. As a result, both were imbued with self-reliance and professionalism that few of their friends possessed.

At 400 Park Avenue, the entrance hall was a mannered study in high contrast and perfect scale. Ebonized floors reflected brilliantly against matte, light-colored walls, while nineteenth-century four-foot-tall blackamoors ceremoniously flanked a door. The clean expanse of walls was punctuated by a Louis XV–style boulle-work clock mounted on a wall bracket, both glinting seductively of gilt and exotic tortoiseshell, and a dark portrait dramatically suspended on a ribbon mount over a door, exaggerating the height of the room. Lacquered doors provided the final note of punch in the tenebrous hall. Like Stacey, Vreeland had a pronounced sense of the baroque balanced by common sense—described by Bill Blass as "a practicality of clean lines, fresh ideas, and relentless professionalism." She evidently loved this shadowy anteroom, a prelude to the effervescent living room, and chose to pose here for fashion photographer George Platt Lynes, decoratively festooned with pearls in homage to her idol Chanel, who "threw ropes of costume jewelry onto everything in this wonderful way."

Blackamoors, holding pride of place in the hall, set the tone for an esoteric style statement. Helped along by inclusion in *Harper's Bazaar*'s 1938 forecast of coming style trends, blackamoors, already fashionable in

Stacey and Vreeland shared a pronounced sense of the baroque balanced by common sense—described by Bill Blass as "a practicality of clean lines, fresh ideas, and relentless professionalism." At 400 Park Avenue, the entrance hall was a mannered study in high style, high contrast, and perfect scale.

Paris, were stirred as a trend in the United States by Stacey and Vreeland. As with all classics, the blackamoor sentries, as well as nearly every object Stacey placed in 400 Park Avenue, endured. Vreeland retained these pieces to the end of her life, moving them to her next apartment at 550 Park Avenue; ultimately, they would end up in Sotheby's sale of her estate in 1990.

The living room held forth like Diana Vreeland herself, demanding attention with its theatrical presence. Stacey loved mirrors and used them repeatedly for the glimmer, light, dimension, allure, and ambiguity they contributed to a space. For the Vreeland living room, he installed plate mirror above the sofa as well as over the polychrome mantel, brilliantly draping them to emphasize the stage-set nature of the room. The mirror curtains were solid red, while the window curtains deftly accentuated height with a narrow vertical stripe, both banded with a perky ball fringe rather than a more formal—and expensive—tassel fringe. The sofa and banquette, covered in a print, were piled with pillows and surrounded by tables and small chairs, including insouciant picnic chairs. Another pair of blackamoors—twisting, parcel-gilt fantasies—were utilized as drinks tables.

Stacey, known for skillful wall compositions, added still more mirrors (two Regency convex mirrors and an over-scaled carved mirror with attached brackets holding nacre shells) then jazzed up the walls further with Venetian gilt-wood brackets surmounted with more shells, French crystal sconces, photos, and masses of drawings by Christian Bérard, surrealist and set designer Eugene Berman, and others in the most nonchalant of arrangements. In appreciation of the dizzying array of mirrors and gilt on her walls, Vreeland made a note in her personal household book about the importance of mirror in a room.

V *reeland's living room held forth like Mrs. Vreeland herself, demanding instantaneous attention with its theatrical presence. Stacey loved mirrors and used them repeatedly to add glimmer, light, dimension, allure, and ambiguity to a room. For the Vreeland living room, he installed plate mirror above the sofa as well as over the polychrome mantel, brilliantly draping them to emphasize the stage-set nature of the room. The theatrical nature of Stacey's work easily lent itself to Vreeland's fashion shoots for* Harper's Bazaar.

Untitled, March 1941, Photograph by Louise Dahl-Wolfe

"Nine Months in a Chinese Jacket" was Vreeland's title for a Harper's Bazaar story on maternity clothes, and it still is a brilliantly inventive formula for negotiating pregnancy with style (although in retrospect, the cigarette doesn't seem such an inspired idea). Stacey's equally brilliant improvisation in Vreeland's living room included rattan picnic chairs cheekily holding their own with blackamoors.

S tacey hung both a serpentine Regency convex mirror and a carved mirror with brackets in the Vreeland living room then further jazzed up the wall with gilt-wood brackets surmounted by nacre shells. While Vreeland duly recorded in her household notebook the importance of mirrors in a room, photographer Louise Dahl-Wolfe cast the shell-filled corner as a languorous seraglio for a Harper's Bazaar fashion shoot.

GEORGE STACEY AND THE CREATION OF AMERICAN CHIC

I n her famous "Why Don't You…" column, Vreeland encouraged readers to stop being boring and create some interest in their lives, and her apartment by Stacey followed suit, rising triumphantly above undistinguished architecture and limited means to exude stylish sophistication.

Like all classics, nearly every object and idea Stacey utilized in 400 Park Avenue endured. Vreeland retained these pieces to the end of her life. Above, Vreeland reclines at 550 Park Avenue, surrounded by Stacey furniture and a festooned mirror, a Stacey device that Billy Baldwin repurposed when asked to create for Vreeland a "garden in hell."

Such headiness was counterbalanced by the humble. For the storage of extensive memorabilia, papers, and accessories, Stacey nimbly shifted from stylist to down-to-earth space planner, devising for Vreeland a banquette of cushions over modular storage pieces, as well as a matching desk vaguely reminiscent of campaign furniture (and uncannily suggestive of a tip from her column: "Why Don't You...build in a bunk like Shirley Temple's in *Captain January* with drawers underneath for clothes and toys?") Meanwhile, books spilled out of simply constructed bookcases.

The room was of the moment, it caught the eye, and, as Stacey rooms so often did, it pleased the camera. With its seductive profiles, cozy corners, spatial ambiguity, contrasting tonalities, sparkle of mirror, gilt, nacre, and originality, the room was catnip for photographers. The most august and elegant fashion photographers—George Hoyningen-Huene and Louise Dahl-Wolfe—shot the room perfectly accessorized with lithe models decorating the sofa, banquette, and mantel. George Platt Lynes also captured the fresh-faced fashion editor center stage in her drawing room, leaning confidently against her draped mirror, displaying her signature snood and layers of costume necklaces.

Diana Vreeland's bedroom contained more conventional luxuries—a fashionable upholstered sleigh bed, deeply curtained windows, a tidy upholstered chair, and daintily wallpapered walls. These revealed a private, conservative side to Vreeland, who respected old-fashioned good manners, believed in the proper running of a home, and maintained detailed household and entertaining notebooks. Still, the inflection in the bedroom is rather more Mayfair than Manhattan, with its sensual fur coverlet, leopard throw pillow, and fine-boned occasional table. It seems the faux-fur elements used by Stacey for this room prompted another suggestion for *Harper's Bazaar* readers: "Why Don't You... go to [a] theatrical-material shop and get fake leopard skin?" As for the coverlet, it too seems the source for another practical Vreeland tip: toss a white monkey fur mounted on yellow velvet on your bed.

The decorating momentum engendered by Stacey's and Vreeland's efforts in the city soon extended to the Vreelands' country house. The three-story converted stable on the property of Reed Vreeland's father in Brewster, New York, was transformed into what Diana Vreeland deemed "by far and away the most romantic country house you could ever imagine." For once, she was not speaking in hyperbole. Sophistication tempered by budget, practicality, and independence provided a platform for invention and fantasy on which Vreeland and Stacey combined dissimilar, dramatic, and cozy elements into a happy family setting. Again, Stacey was blessed with providential client connections: on weekends, the Vreelands hosted Kitty Bache Miller (who would also hire Stacey), Louise Macy—*Harper's Bazaar*'s former Paris editor, former girlfriend of Jock Whitney, and now married to Franklin Roosevelt's éminence grise, Harry Hopkins—Edward Warburg, Elsa Schiaparelli, and jewelers Fulco di Verdura and Jean Schlumberger (coincidentally Frances Cheney's pet jeweler). A designer could not have hired a better publicist.

The color-saturated living room was inevitably a high-style statement of country living. Stacey treated the double-height great room like the interior of a box, painting it entirely—inclusive of trim and ceiling—an unheard of cyclamen pink. At a time when most homes exhibited gentle pastels and modulated neutrals, the shock of walls audaciously enameled the signature color of Elsa Schiaparelli must have provided

---

The apartment Stacey designed for Vreeland took a modern approach to decorating, adapting convention to suit new circumstances. For the storage of extensive memorabilia, papers, and accessories (opposite, top), Stacey nimbly shifted from stylist to down-to-earth space planner, devising for Vreeland a banquette of cushions over modular storage pieces (seen in photo on page 70), as well as a desk vaguely reminiscent of campaign furniture. Ever inspired by improvisation, Vreeland penned, "Why Don't You...build a bunk like Shirley Temple's in Captain January *with drawers underneath for clothes and toys?"*

Diana Vreeland's bedroom (opposite, bottom) contained traditional luxuries—a fashionable upholstered sleigh bed, deeply curtained windows, a tidy upholstered chair, and daintily wallpapered walls—that revealed a private, conservative side to Vreeland, who respected old-fashioned good manners, believed in the proper running of a home, and maintained detailed household and entertaining notebooks. Stacey's faux-fur additions inspired Vreeland to query Harper's Bazaar *readers: "Why Don't You...go to a theatrical-material shop and get fake leopard skin?" The fur coverlet prompted another Vreeland tip: toss a white monkey fur mounted on yellow velvet on your bed.*

GEORGE STACEY AND THE CREATION OF AMERICAN CHIC

"Far and away the most romantic country house you could ever imagine" was Diana Vreeland's description of her country house in Brewster. The color-saturated living room (left) was undoubtedly a high-style statement of country living. Stacey treated the double-height great room as the interior of a box, painting it entirely—inclusive of trim and ceiling—an unheard-of cyclamen pink.

Stacey, always enamored with classical form, placed a simple white urn lamp that contrasted smartly with the Schiaparelli pink walls of Vreeland's living room (above). The bearskin rug simply begged for a fashion shoot of lacey lingerie.

The Metropolitan Museum of Art

SPECIAL CONSULTANT

April 16th, 1973

George —

Nothing gave me more pleasure than getting your letter, George.

I cannot get over the fact that you are here living in America and that you came down to the Museum to see our Balenciaga show.

Curiously enough I had no thought of the bedroom doors on the balcony at Brewster but now that you speak of it, perhaps I had it at the back of my mind! However, the colors in the show are the colors of Balenciaga which I noted from the fabricant in Zurich.

I could not be more pleased that you liked the show and curiously enough it seems to please a lot of people which is great. You were marvellous to write to me and I got a big kick out of hearing from you.

always my love

Diana Vreeland.

Diana

George Stacey
110 East 57th Street
New York City, N.Y 10022

At a time when most homes exhibited gentle pastels and modulated neutrals, the shock of walls painted the signature color of Elsa Schiaparelli provided endless streams of conversation. A large balcony that overhung the living room introduced another daring innovation—every door was enameled a different bright color. Years later, keen colorists Stacey and Vreeland were still musing via correspondence (above) about the door colors. Stacey postulated that their choice of colors subliminally channeled the palette of the great Cristóbal Balenciaga. Vreeland's Balenciaga exhibit at the Metropolitan Museum (opposite) lends a clue to the colors of the balcony doors.

endless streams of conversation. A large balcony that overhung the living room introduced another daring innovation—every door was enameled a different bright color. Years later and long after the Brewster house had been sold, keen colorists Stacey and Vreeland were still musing via correspondence about the door colors, Stacey postulating that their choice of colors subliminally channeled the palette of the great Cristóbal Balenciaga, who had opened his atelier in Paris in 1937, slightly before Stacey and Vreeland tackled the country house decorating.

Paired with the vivid palette was a relaxed and open furniture arrangement centered around the fireplace that included plenty of stools and pull-up chairs, as well as those handy rattan picnic chairs, masses of throw pillows, magazines, and baskets heaped with firewood, all intended to invite lingering, reading, and conversation. In a corner stood a dining table surrounded by Hepplewhite chairs. The banquette idea from 400 Park Avenue—modular storage and all—proved so successful that it was adopted for the country-house living room as well (and still later at 550 Park Avenue, designed by Billy Baldwin). Pattern and texture exerted itself in Bessarabian, bearskin, and hooked rugs, as well as a dense, colorful hollyhock chintz. Counterintuitively, Stacey reined in the profusion of elements and color with assertive color, creating coherence by wrapping the room in a strong, uniform hue. Stacey, always enamored with classical form, placed a white urn lamp on a table and simple urn vases on the mantel. Sober curtains offset by an austere portrait further disciplined the room.

Unlike the suave bedroom at 400 Park Avenue, the country-house bedroom was a romantic fantasy. The airy room was dominated by a diaphanous canopy allegedly more than twenty feet high topped by a medieval-Victorian tufted velvet pelmet; the linens were printed with butterflies, the petticoat of a lampshade—on a classical urn base—was decked out in organdy ruffles. The bedside table's witty black-and-white base was repeated in the silhouetted profiles of Vreeland's beloved sons hanging on the wall above. Modern low-backed slipper chairs with exposed legs again revealed a romantic streak—button tufting and eyelet-and-ribbon antimacassars—and along with the pelmet announced Stacey's developing interest in Victoriana.

Again, with its contrasts of vivid prints, light and dark, strong profiles, and arresting objects, the house in Brewster was a natural location for photo shoots. Louise Dahl-Wolfe, the most baroque photographer of her day, with a hawk's eye for profile, composition, and negative space (incidentally, Dahl-Wolfe had trained as an interior designer as well as a photographer), recorded these interiors for *Harper's Bazaar* in the early 1940s. Whether showcasing svelte evening dresses, wartime country living, filmy lingerie, or Vreeland herself, Stacey's interiors for Vreeland tight-roped the line between practical reality and inventive fancy. And, as was the case for all of Stacey's work, the design highlighted the individual who inhabited these rooms rather than a designer signature.

U̶nlike the suave Vreeland bedroom at 400 Park Avenue, the country bedroom
was a romantic fantasy. The airy room was dominated by a diaphanous canopy
topped by a medieval-Victorian tufted velvet pelmet. Modern low-backed slipper chairs
with exposed legs, button tufting, and eyelet-and-ribbon antimacassars underscore the
romanticism of the room—and signal Stacey's growing interest in Victoriana.

Neither Vreeland nor Stacey shied away from the simple. In the master bedroom, hyacinths in humble pots top a fanciful shell fireplace, while a model reclines on banquette cushions placed on the floor. Although Stacey could and did fall for many a grand Coromandel screen and signed bergère, he exhibited a careless indifference to ostentatiously grand rooms.

CHAPTER SIX

THEME AND VARIATIONS

1936–1942

Amidst the swirls of glamour, George Stacey pursued a new muse. While stylish classicism would remain consistently at the heart of his vision, Stacey's aesthetic curiosity dictated forays into new design territory. By the late 1930s, Stacey was smitten with Victoriana, which he smartly reinterpreted. In accents in Diana Vreeland's country bedroom, the Victorian elements are light and charming. A more broad experiment with faux bamboo and furbelows was, appropriately, conducted under the aegis of Frances Cheney's latest brainstorm, The Decorators Picture Gallery.

From the very beginning, Frances' gallery on Madison Avenue was a sensation. Working alongside her sister, Alice Gates, Cheney had matched her flair with an innovative concept—exhibiting fine art in the context of actual rooms. No less an art personage than Conger Goodyear, president of the Museum of Modern Art, presided over the 1936 opening of The Decorators Picture Gallery, while *ARTnews*, *The New Yorker*, and *The New York Times* avidly covered exhibits mounted by the gallery. Prestigious art

dealers, such as Jacques Seligmann and Wildenstein & Company, perceiving the commercial possibilities in such an enterprise, lent Impressionist, post-Impressionist, old master, and contemporary paintings to the gallery (which also claimed exclusive representation of Giorgio de Chirico), while fashionable decorators, including McMillen, Arthur Vernay, Tate and Hall, Jansen, and James Pendleton—possibly persuaded by the great Eleanor Lambert, who handled the publicity—queued up to design vignettes to showcase the art. Working with three Henri de Toulouse-Lautrec portraits for an exhibit in 1938, Stacey caused a small stir when he assembled faux bamboo, potted plants, flocked damask wallpaper, gilt-wood cupids, and a swagged velvet wainscot into a verging-on-camp Belle Époque "cocktail room."

But more fun than designing flip cocktail rooms was an elegant new project for the Cheneys. In the late 1930s, Frances and Ward Cheney found a Fifth Avenue apartment suffused with light and graced with Central Park views and a pretty stairwell—a happy contrast to the dark formality and awkward layout of their Elsie Cobb Wilson–designed apartment. George Stacey, of course, was called in to decorate the new space, and by the time the decade came to a close—Frances Cheney's daughter's last memory of the old apartment was listening to the king's speech on the kitchen radio in September 1939—Stacey had produced an apartment that captured once again the charm of the Cheneys and the worldliness of the era.

Like The Decorators Picture Gallery, the new Cheney apartment was a media sensation. Diana Vreeland, universally acknowledged for her talent at conceptualizing great fashion photographs, twice staged *Harper's Bazaar* fashion shoots with her glamour photographer of choice, Louise Dahl-Wolfe, in the apartment. *Town & Country* published the apartment as a design story, accompanied by photographs by Hans van Nes. Fascinated by the opulent bath with satin sofa and Louis XVI chauffeuse, *Vogue* featured the room as a sybaritic alternative to the functional bathrooms of the day.

Although Stacey made it look easy (and it probably *was* easy working for such seemingly delightful clients), designing for the Cheneys required special skill. Like Stacey's other great client of the era, Diana Vreeland, Frances Cheney radiated unlimited confidence, inspiration, and energy, but there was a noteworthy difference—Mrs. Cheney had a seemingly endless supply

*I*n the new Cheney living room, a rug of rustic string contrasted provocatively with soigné velvet, silks, and satins. The Cheneys hung a Renoir over the mantel and a de Chirico over the canapé. Amidst this glittery cocktail, Stacey had the good sense to leave expanses of wall unadorned, which made the objects and art all the more dramatic.

of money. While the challenge with the Vreelands was to work magic out of relatively thin air, the trick with the Cheneys was quite the opposite: to edit and to stay focused when faced with infinite tantalizing possibilities. Though by no means a style curmudgeon, Stacey brought the necessary judicious eye to the project: the new apartment, while stylish and dramatic, was underscored by an inherent poise.

But the elegance was not just any elegance. It was inventive elegance—and like their Locust Valley country house and the Vreeland residences, the apartment mapped out new design territory. It was not only the

Stacey's focus on volume, symmetry, structure, and balance lent modernity to a living room populated with antiques. As in the Vreeland country house, designed at roughly the same time, Stacey contained the broad sweep of decorative periods and provenances in the Cheney living room in an envelope of strong color, making dissimilar objects look perfectly natural together.

"Untitled," March 1941; Photograph by Louise Dahl-Wolfe

T own & Country *asserted that Stacey was "a radical in velvet" after he upholstered architectural trim in the Cheney apartment (including doors and pagoda-shaped pediments) in gray-blue velvet. When Diana Vreeland staged a fashion shoot in the apartment, Louise Dahl-Wolfe posed a model in a surreal cage ruff against the extraordinary door gesturing to a Venetian mirror and gilt-wood console in the hallway beyond.*

Untitled," March 1941, Photograph by Louise Dahl-Wolfe

The impudence of a flounced skirt paired with ladylike white gloves is equally matched by Stacey's tossing a modern chair (attributed to René Drouet) into an antique-filled room. Mirrored window reveals, an overscaled Venetian mirror, Italian gilt-wood, satin upholstery, and extravagantly dangling crystals dancing against the navy walls supplied the requisite sparkle.

colors and the periods of the furniture that were new, it was also the approach ("The concept!" we imagine Vreeland roaring as she arrived with her crew for a fashion shoot). For the apartment was not simply about stuff (although there was plenty of that, and it was all good), it was equally defined by the absence of stuff—scale, negative space, light, and proportion—and daring. When the focus *did* shift to things, one found a collection of vastly dissimilar objects, mostly antique, that nevertheless managed to look perfectly natural together.

Stacey's focus on volume, symmetry, structure, and balance lends a living room populated with antiques unexpected modernity. As in the Vreeland country house designed at roughly the same time, Stacey contained the broad sweep of decorative periods and provenances in the Cheney living room in an envelope of strong color. The room was night blue—matching Frances' eyes—with flashes of rose, gilt, and mirror. Still thinking of a room as "the interior of a box," Stacey tinted the ceiling blue and, completely justifying *Town & Country*'s assertion that he was "a radical in velvet," experimented with upholstering architectural trim, including doors, pagoda-shaped pediments, and all moldings, in gray-blue velvet. (The chinoiserie pelmets and curtains were also made of the same blue velvet.) The other components of the room, in lighter colors, stood in dramatic relief against the dark walls. A rug of natural string, nearly as large as the room, lightened the palette, its rustic texture contrasting provocatively with soigné velvet, silks, and satins. As with many innovations, it was delightfully original but not yet perfected: Frankie's daughter remembers that the maid had to exit the room backwards to collect all the straying strings.

Stacey had culled furniture with prominent profiles—ranging from an Italian gilt-wood bench to a mother-of-pearl inlaid Japanese low table and Louis XVI chair and what looks like a gilded Drouet chair in the foreground—to sit in bas-relief against the dark walls. The glimmer of the Baltic chandelier, mirrored window reveals, an overscaled Venetian mirror (reflecting yet another mirror), Italian gilt wood, satin upholstery, and modern crystal rod lamps animates the serene, shadowy space. The Cheneys hung a Renoir over the mantel and a de Chirico over the canapé. Amidst this glittery cocktail, Stacey had the good sense to leave expanses of wall unadorned, which simply made the beautiful objects all the more effective.

Throughout his career, Stacey wrestled with the traditional dining room. For the Cheney house in Locust Valley, he simply dispensed with the room, allowing alfresco dining to suffice in the *belle saison* or a table set up by the fireplace to be used in the cooler months, a rather radical notion in the realm of Locust Valley (and rectified by later owners of the house). In other projects, he paired small tables with low-slung banquettes or integrated a dining table into the living room, as he did for the Vreelands in Brewster. In the new Cheney apartment, he retained a dining room but overturned all conventions about dining and entertaining, placing small tufted banquettes lavished with fringe and pillbox pillows of cut velvet around the perimeter of the room for cozy dining against mirrored walls festooned with gold damask swags and jabots. (It is hard to know whether Frances Cheney or Diana Vreeland got the stage-set mirror treatment first.) Expanding on the concept he

While no one can now recall whether Stacey was inspired by the mirrors of a Venetian ridotto or the fashionable club El Morocco (whose owner claimed New Yorkers' favorite entertainment was watching themselves), one fact is undisputed: Stacey's nightclub-style dining room for Frances and Ward Cheney epitomized Café Society glamour. Characteristically infusing Old World elements with of-the-moment sass, Stacey blended parcel-gilt Italian chairs, a Baltic chandelier, and gilt girandoles with layers of mirror.

used at The Decorators Picture Gallery, Stacey replaced the predictable long table with a series of small tables, some with reflective surfaces, others made of gilded faux bamboo hung with tiny bell pendants (reutilized after their debut in The Decorators Picture Gallery vignette).

The colors and lighting of this room are mysterious and glamorous, with marigold damask glistening against smoky silvery walls and mirrors. Gilt and glass further the collective shimmer: Louis XV branched candelabrum (again, those tall candles noted by Albert Hadley), Italian parcel gilt chairs, Louis XVI armchairs covered in reflective silvery brocade, and a Baltic chandelier punctuate the room with light. Towering screens set with mirrors soften corners, adding stature as well as ambiguity; sober fluted pedestals contribute gravitas. Perhaps Stacey was channeling a Venetian ridotto, or

"Untitled," March 1941; Photograph by Louise Dahl-Wolfe

A poised master of mirror tricks and wall composition, Stacey arranged watercolors, needlework, and drawings to reflect in a café table in the Cheney dining room. As part of Stacey's quest to reinvent the conventional dining room, mirrored tables would also appear in dining rooms in Hobe Sound and Sands Point for the Averell Harrimans. Note the gilt-wood bells dangling from the table.

P laying type against type, delicate lace tambours demurred under tailored window curtains and a rustic string rug offset the silky femininity of the Cheney bedroom. Stacey introduced the all-important note of black with papier-mâché chairs. The editors of Town & County sardonically commented: "Give us o Lord our daily platitude can never be written about Frances Cheney or her decorator George Stacey."

perhaps the nightclub El Morocco, whose owner, John Perona, astutely noted that the favorite entertainment of New Yorkers was observing themselves. A Steinway sat in the corner, waiting for the dinner parties when the Cheneys hired a pianist to play Gershwin and Cole Porter tunes in their seductive supper club of a dining room. (The beautiful chanteuse Maxine Sullivan, famous for her swing version of "Loch Lomond," was Ward Cheney's particular favorite.)

Frances Cheney's confidence in her decorator released unbounded creativity in Stacey, producing more otherworldly results in the master bedroom. There, a mirrored ceiling (studded with rosettes as at Versailles) mesmerized the lens of Louise Dahl-Wolfe in a fashion shoot for *Harper's Bazaar* and mortified Anne Cheney Zinsser, who noted that none of her Brearley classmates' parents had a bedroom with a similar ceiling. But as Stacey and Frances Cheney had wagered (who knows what Ward Cheney thought of all of this), the

A mirrored ceiling in the Cheney master bedroom (studded with rosettes in homage to Versailles) mesmerized the lens of Louise Dahl-Wolfe in a fashion shoot for Harper's Bazaar—and mortified daughter Anne Cheney Zinsser, who noted that none of her Brearley classmates' parents had a bedroom with a similar ceiling.

effect was dramatic and luminous. For the bed canopy, Stacey imaginatively created a valance and curtain of long, twisted cords—a kind of bullion fringe on steroids—rather than a typical pretty fabric. Playing type against type again, delicate lace tambours demurred under tailored window curtains. A papier-mâché chair inlaid with mother-of-pearl introduced the elegant desirable note of black advocated by Diana Vreeland in her "Why Don't You…" column. A rug, of the same impractical, extraordinary, and tactile string as the living room rug, covered the floor, surely leaving the poor maid in tears. From the ceiling, Stacey suspended a beaded crystal chandelier, its sheathed silk stem doubled in length by its reflection in the mirror. "'Give us O Lord our daily platitude' can never be written about Frances Cheney or her decorator George Stacey," concluded *Town & Country*.

The spirit of Malmaison reigned in Frances Cheney's bath and dressing room, which Stacey swathed in white

silk, adding quick strokes of black, shots of gilt for smartness, and a pale blue sofa for indulgence. Again, a mirror featured prominently in the design, mounted along one wall and covering a dressing table. *Vogue* wrote that with its mirror and chic black scatter rugs on the dark floor (and a special drawer for exercise books), the room could double as a private gymnasium. Perhaps one *could* manage a few sit-ups gazing at the pale blue ceiling, but the delicate boudoir seems more conducive to the pursuits of a modern Josephine: sipping tea on a low Louis XVI slipper chair in front of the fire, lingering à la Marat in the theatrically curtained bath, or assessing a new Vionnet gown in a mirror revealed by a clever tying back of the silk wall hangings.

In the Cheney apartment, Stacey quickly refined the literal Victorian references from The Decorators Picture Gallery into a cool stylishness of his own making. While Syrie Maugham incorporated Victorian touches that were feminine and fanciful, in Stacey's hands, the outdated and overstuffed Victorian elements became smart and sensuous: an old-fashioned *borne* in the Cheney living room was sophisticatedly squared off and trimmed with overscaled tasseled fringe; the tufted banquettes in the Cheney dining room were far more sexy than stodgy; and the tufted slipper chair in the Vreeland country bedroom was neatly updated with exposed tapered, rather than turned, legs. And although stylized and modified, Stacey's rediscovery of the nineteenth century was news. "What I can hardly wait to see is the Edwardian cocktail room which George Stacey will do around Toulouse-Lautrec paintings," one art critic wrote breathlessly about Stacey's vignette for The Decorators Picture Gallery, proudly adding her big scoop: "I have seen the flock paper he is going to use." Soon other significant designers were also dabbling in Victoriana. A 1939 issue of *Harper's Bazaar* reported that the noted West Coast decorator Frances Elkins had placed a Victorian tufted settee in the Yerba Buena Club in San Francisco.

But all was not focused on the merits of tufting. In writing of Stacey's cocktail room at The Decorators Picture Gallery, *Vogue* pointed out the mismatch between a cocktail room, "a witty comment on decoration," and the era. Somber developments across the Atlantic would soon make phenomena such as graceful cocktail rooms, household staffs that picked strings off shedding carpets, chanteuses at private dinner parties, and Vionnet gowns quaint relics of a vanished time.

CHAPTER SEVEN

THE SMART SET AT WAR

1942–1945

The easy inventiveness Stacey displayed for Frances Cheney and Diana Vreeland in the 1930s slipped into composed classicism for Astors, Mortimers, Phippses, and Whitneys during the war years. Experimental string rugs, witty sculptural profiles, and imaginative flights of fancy yielded to a darkening palette in rooms that now provided reassuring comfort. In accordance with the sober times, Stacey rationed his stylish statements; the decorator who loved drama, French furniture, and disciplined chic censored his more baroque leanings while demonstrating an ability to work discreetly in the background.

The change of atmosphere brought more bibelots, framed pictures, personal objects, and even English furniture into Stacey's rooms, much to the pleasure of new clients Minnie Astor, Betsey Whitney, and Babe Mortimer—the glamorous Cushing sisters described by Billy Baldwin as holding a monopoly on taste. While hallmarks of the Stacey aesthetic—scale, color, contrast, and sparkle—still threaded their way through the new sedate rooms, they only reached high gear in Stacey's own residences of the era: an East Side

While projects for the Vreelands and Cheneys had established Stacey as the decorator of the young fashionable set, designing for the Astors carried a whiff of the Four Hundred and introduced a note of grown-up seriousness to Stacey's client list. Though not as decorous as their forebears assembled in their Gilded Age living room (above), Minnie and Vincent Astor looked to Stacey for sedate English-inspired interiors enlivened by Stacey's use of saturated color.

Given the artistic leanings of Minnie Astor and Stacey, it is hardly surprising that there was a quirky undertone to the mahogany and chintz interiors of the Astor apartment at 120 East End Avenue. Minnie Astor (opposite), a bohemian in Mainbocher, was later known for her literary and artistic salon.

apartment that is mysterious, layered, and sophisticated and a country house that may be the most glamorous adaptive-reuse project on record.

As Stacey's client list was lengthening, the clipping file expanded with notable connections and projects. Besides the highly visible Cushing sisters, Diana Vreeland's friend Kitty Bache Miller would hire Stacey. (What is one person's delight is another's bane, as this situation would prove. While Vreeland found inspiration in improvisation and bargains and Frances Cheney loved aesthetic adventure, Miller approached decorating very seriously and was frustrated by Stacey's reverse chic, leading her to complain that his thrifty fabric selections were unworthy of her.) Probably much more interesting to Stacey was Edward Warburg, who possessed an art collection with works by Pablo Picasso, Henri Matisse, Georgia O'Keeffe, and Constantin Brancusi and connections to the ballet and art world. *Vogue* photographed Stacey's clients Mrs. Townsend Martin and Mrs. Averell Harriman in Stacey-designed rooms and reported that the William Harknesses were also clients. Somewhere along the way, Stacey's name was also associated with the beautiful Mona Williams.

The patronage of the Vreelands and Cheneys established Stacey as the decorator of the young and fashionable, but it was the Astor name with its suggestion of the old New York Four Hundred that introduced a note of seriousness to Stacey's client list. The decorating was pretty serious, too. After donating his yacht to the government, Vincent Astor closed his Rhinebeck country house, Ferncliff, with its famous Stanford White playhouse, joined the U.S. Navy, and left his bride Minnie Cushing—a sophisticated city girl, later known for a literary and artistic salon—to redecorate the apartment at 120 East End Avenue. Minnie, a design independent who liked bright colors, chintz, and inviting rooms (to the dismay of her successor, Brooke Astor) hired the decorator known for his eye for color, who in turn produced a polished retreat so personal and welcoming that it easily compensated for an unavailable country house. While Stacey reused much of the Astors' furniture, which happened to be English, its use in part reflected the affinity Americans felt for the English then engaged in heroic battle across the Atlantic.

But in spite of mahogany and chintz and sentiment, there was something not conventionally English about the Astor apartment. There was a light touch of the

At the onset of the war, Vincent Astor donated his yacht for government use, closed his country houses, and joined the Navy, while Minnie volunteered for the Ships Service Committee and the Henry Street Settlement visiting nurses campaigns. For the hardworking Astors and others who dedicated themselves to the war effort, homes became personal havens rather than glamorous stage sets.

Though, as *Vogue* noted admiringly, the Astor apartment displayed an English country house sensibility, Stacey tucked in a few notes of New World flair. A light touch of the baroque, the confidence to leave space elegantly spare and walls unadorned, exaggerated proportions, vivid contrasts, and smart profiles spiced up restrained interiors. Next to a table covered in ruby-red damask, Minnie Astor and her dachshund Robin Hood sit on a sabre-leg settee (opposite), its antique white frame sharply silhouetted against the dark wall.

Rose damask, a Venetian mirror, sparkling crystal sconces, and gilded picture frames reveal the hand of Stacey in Minnie Astor's emerald living room (above, right). Somewhat later, the wall color was changed to cornflower blue.

Reflecting America's sympathy for the principled English, Anglomania surged. The Astor library (below, right), filled with bibelots, books, deep-seated upholstery, and polished mahogany, offered a reassuring retreat.

In contrast to the sober library, Minnie Astor's bedroom (above) with a duchesse brisée, a Louis XVI console, a fashionable contemporary screen commissioned from Marcel Vertès (for years a cover illustrator for Harper's Bazaar) and a boldly tasseled bed canopy was nearly antebellum in its French femininity. Blue and white chintz used for the curtains, chaise longue, and bed dressings serenely unifies the room.

Stacey confidently featured austerity in the Astors' guest bedroom (opposite), strictly limiting the color scheme to a powdery gray blue and bois de rose, applying white panel moldings to unembellished walls, and grounding the whole with a faded Aubusson rug. The room exuded Stacey discipline and understatement. The few painted Louis XV and Directoire pieces are perfectly scaled and placed; a black lacquer coffee table offers contrast to the pastel palette. The delicate patterning of shadow and light provides the most refined, and ephemeral, of ornaments.

baroque, the confidence to leave space elegantly spare and walls unadorned, relieved by only the occasional fine painting, and an interest in exaggerating height, exercising contrast, and emphasizing profile against color that is thoroughly New World. Mannerisms of the Stacey style show up in Minnie Astor's velvety emerald green and chintz living room with the use of rose damask, a Venetian mirror, sparkling crystal sconces, the silhouette of a white Regency settee, gilded picture frames, attention to profile, and, of course, saturated color. And as if it could not have been otherwise, Stacey introduced a French note, a single Louis XVI chair, a symbolic lonely representative of the Free French amidst the sea of English furniture.

In contrast, Minnie's pale blue bedroom with a duchesse brisée, a Louis XVI console, and boldly tasseled bed canopy is nearly antebellum in its unabashed femininity. As at the Vreelands', Stacey matter-of-factly used antiques for modern purposes while adding a fashionable contemporary screen commissioned from Marcel Vertès (for years a cover illustrator for Harper's Bazaar). The room is filled with books, photos, and the necessities of a busy and meaningful life, all of which Stacey neatly confined to designated surfaces (bureau

top, bedside tables), minimizing clutter and ensuring an elegant backdrop to show off fine *objets* and carvings.

While Minnie's room was convivial, Stacey confidently featured austerity in the guest bedroom, strictly limiting the color scheme to a powdery gray blue and bois de rose, applying white panel moldings to unembellished walls, laying a faded Aubusson rug, and excising any frivolous objects. The room exuded Stacey discipline and understatement: the few painted Louis XV and Directoire pieces are perfectly scaled, placed, and selected; a black lacquer coffee table offered contrast to the pastel palette. Within the strict formality, the graceful duchesse canopy was a salient note of softness, and with few accessories, the delicate patterning of shadow and light provided the most refined, and ephemeral, of ornaments.

As the Cushing sisters often operated in concert, it was hardly surprising that when Betsey Cushing Roosevelt married sportsman, theatrical producer, Selznick partner, art collector, and all-around gentleman Jock Whitney, she, too, turned to Stacey. Whereas Minnie with her artistic leanings was a bohemian in Mainbocher, Betsey was the quintessential lady, an accomplished hostess and devoted wife. Stacey fully understood that both Betsey and Jock Whitney, two highly secure individuals, did not wish anything like a signature style. They knew exactly what they wanted—comfortable elegance, a feeling of leisure, quiet luxury, nothing overdone—as did Stacey, who despite wartime shortages pulled off a discreet but sumptuous apartment for the Whitneys that was full of flowers, deep tufted upholstery, and, gloriously, Renoir's *Bal du Moulin de la Galette*, casually purchased by Jock Whitney one afternoon after lunch. With Jock away in the war (like Astor, he turned his yacht over for government use and obtained an officers' commission), Betsey Whitney posed with her two daughters for *Vogue* in a dress with a ruffled neckline evocative of a figure in an eighteenth-century English portrait by Thomas Gainsborough (if not Betsy Ross). The dress was a far cry from the 1930s glamour-girl garb so blithely worn by Frances Cheney and Diana Vreeland and in complete accordance with the conservative fashion of the times, as was the green and red living room.

All three sisters had warm relations with their decorator. *House & Garden* documented the friendship of Minnie Astor and George Stacey in a story about clients

Stacey fully understood that Betsey and Jock Whitney, two highly secure individuals, did not wish anything like a signature decorator style. They knew exactly what they wanted—quiet luxury, nothing overdone—as did Stacey, who, despite wartime shortages, pulled off a discreet apartment (opposite) full of flowers, deep tufted upholstery, and, gloriously, Renoir's Bal du Moulin de la Galette.

Babe Cushing (below), at the time a fashion editor at Vogue, *hired Stacey to decorate her brownstone apartment when she married Stanley Mortimer. For a first apartment on a relative budget, Stacey fashioned red, green, and white rooms around inherited family pieces and then, as if on a religious mission, spent hours with Babe hunting for the odd antique, object, and bauble for the perfect finish.*

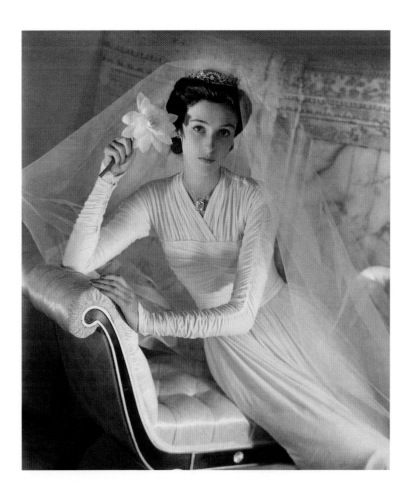

and color, while Betsey Whitney, late in life, would invite George to lunch at Greentree, her country house, offering to send her car. But it was with the legendary Babe that Stacey had the most profound connection, for they shared an unrequited passion for antiques—or perhaps, more precisely, for *antiquing*, as they adored the pursuit of beautiful objects as much as the possession. At the time a fashion editor at *Vogue*, Babe first hired Stacey to help decorate her brownstone triplex apartment when she was married to Stanley Mortimer, then at the advertising firm Ruth, Roth and Ryan (known to his Racquet Club cronies as "Riff, Raff and Ruin"). For a first apartment on a relative budget, Stacey fashioned red, green, and white rooms around inherited family pieces and then, as if on a religious mission, spent hours with Babe hunting for the odd antique, object, and bauble to serve as the perfect finishing effects. Babe particularly adored antique enamels,

I n keeping with wartime mores, Mrs. Townsend Martin appears as lovely, measured, and responsible as her George Stacey–designed house. While Mr. Martin, a grandson of Henry Phipps and winner of the Jockey Club Gold Cup, was away at war, Mrs. Martin was surrounded by timeless symbols of stability: two charming sons, a docile Labrador, beautifully bound books, and English antiques. But a happy little refrain punched through the seriousness: Stacey laced the house with continuity via a veritable flower garden of English chintzes—classic roses, delphinium, larkspur, and camellias, each printed on a fresh white background, define each room.

china, and ornate bottles. Over years of antiquing in New York and Paris with Stacey, Babe gleaned considerable knowledge of French furniture, and she acquired several sets of signed Louis XVI chairs in her own right.

Youthful spirits were one of the many casualties of war. In her photograph in *Vogue*, the very pretty Mrs. Townsend B. Martin wears a simple gingham dress even more modest than that of Betsey Whitney. Despite her fresh loveliness, Mrs. Martin appears measured and responsible, as is her George Stacey–designed house. Indeed, both are superb exemplars of their type: the house and the chatelaine are immaculate, shining, and straightforward. While Mr. Martin, a grandson of Henry Phipps and two-time winner of the Jockey Club Gold Cup, was away on active duty with the Coast Guard, Mrs.

Martin was surrounded by symbols of timeless stability: two charming sons, a docile Labrador retriever, beautifully bound books, and English antiques. But a happy little refrain punches through the seriousness: Stacey laces the house with continuity via a veritable flower garden of English chintzes—classic roses, delphinium, larkspur, and camellia, each printed on a fresh white background, define each room. Ever committed to the cohesive design statement, Stacey even used lively rose chintz for the curtains and the sofa of the paneled library and neatly succeeded: the pretty white fabric contrasts spiritedly with the dark paneling, while the gilded book spines contribute Stacey's signature sparkle.

The war censor, however, seems to have overlooked Stacey's design for the dining room, which stands out for drama reminiscent of Vreeland's foyer. Height is the theme of the room; matte walls, tall baroque-shaped window cornices, and Italian consoles surmounted by enormous dark paintings lead the eye upward. Régence chairs and a rock crystal chandelier have the assurance of prewar design, while Stacey's beloved tall candles teeter everywhere.

Despite extensive design work for his new clients, Stacey found the time to help old friends adapt to changes dictated by wartime shortages of housing and staff. With Ward Cheney serving with the Navy in the South Pacific, Frankie moved with her daughters from her pretty duplex to a temporary flat on East 72nd Street. Deploying scroll consoles and elegant slipper chairs from the old apartment (the bed seems to have gone into storage), Stacey put a brave face on lackluster architecture. While Averell Harriman took off for London to provide Churchill with $42 billion in American aid via the Lend-Lease program, Marie stayed behind to close her beloved art gallery and sort out health issues. Her penthouse on East 68th Street became the site of yet another Stacey experiment in the art of dining. There, he convivially placed low tables in front of an L-configured banquette and improvised a buffet—so handy given wartime staff shortages—from an eighteenth-century console. (Above the console hung Picasso's *Woman with a Fan,* which tidily summed up Marie's predilection for French post-Impressionists.) The stylishly casual room spawned a *Harper's Bazaar* article entitled "The Disappearing Dining Room" and future carefree dining rooms for the Harrimans in Hobe Sound and Sands Point.

Stacey's design for the Townsend Martin dining room stands out for drama, recalling the chiaroscuro effects in Diana Vreeland's foyer. Height is the theme of the room; matte walls, tall window cornices, and Italian consoles surmounted by enormous dark paintings lead the eye upward. Régence chairs and a rock crystal chandelier add prewar assurance to wartime design, while tall candles teeter everywhere.

Marie Harriman, yet another of Stacey's beloved arty beauties, championed post-Impressionist painting in America. After a Parisian honeymoon combining romance with art acquisitions (including, most famously, Van Gogh's White Roses), she launched a gallery on 57th Street that had a glittering opening attended by Henri Matisse. Her 1935 portrait by André Derain (above) is now in the collection of the National Gallery of Art.

Improvising temporary wartime apartments for clients, Stacey put a brave face on the bland architecture resulting from wartime housing shortages. While Averell Harriman flew off to London to administer the Lend-Lease program, Marie Harriman moved to a duplex in New York (opposite) where Degas' Petite Danseuse de Quatorze Ans, a Gauguin, and a Seurat nestled in compact new quarters.

But for all the activity, decorating was not in the forefront of anyone's mind; even fashion magazines like *Harper's Bazaar* recommended savings bonds over scarves for Christmas gifts. ("It strikes an accord among friends who feel deeply…in a year such as this, gifts of trivia are not in order.") War was shifting lives, affecting lifestyles, and dominating thoughts. In addition to clients Harriman, Astor, and Whitney, many in Stacey's close circle were scattering to join the war effort: Ward Cheney, various Davisons, and Artemus Gates, Alice's husband, who resigned the presidency of the New York Trust to serve as Assistant Secretary of the Navy for Air and build up American air power (one of his recruits was Babe Cushing's husband, Stanley Mortimer). Stacey signed up for the Army, as did so many at that dire time.

After a stint as port warden with the Coast Guard and a WPA course in camouflage, Stacey closed his office and entered the army as a first lieutenant. Given his obvious skill with color and draftsmanship, Stacey was naturally assigned to the camouflage office at Fort

Stacey fashioned an offbeat dining room with low tables placed in front of an L-shaped banquette in Marie Harriman's East 68th Street penthouse. An eighteenth-century console with Picasso's Woman with a Fan *hanging over it pinch-hits as a buffet—so handy at a time when staff was hard to come by. The stylishly casual room spawned a* Harper's Bazaar *article, "The Disappearing Dining Room," as well as future nonchalant dining rooms for the Harrimans.*

Belvoir, where he quickly received a promotion. But that went well only when Stacey's work depended solely on technical skills; the new promotion required leadership, stirring up deep-rooted insecurities. Painfully second-guessing himself, unable to direct others, and finding it difficult to concentrate, Stacey spiraled downwards as his carefully constructed ego dissolved. After weeks at Walter Reed Hospital, followed by a diagnosis of psychoneurosis, Stacey was honorably mustered out of the Army and returned, confidence shaken, to New York. Frances Cheney's mother, the flinty Mrs. Davison— patroness of the famed Millionaires' Unit from World War I and mother of government officials and flyboy heroes—immediately sent a sympathetic note to Stacey inviting him to Peacock Point. From that moment, the Davison clan became Stacey's refuge.

With all the Davison men and sons-in-laws involved in the war, the squash court at Peacock Point languished unused. Peacock Point, like almost every location in the United States, sorely missed its men. Mrs. Davison, hoping to bring some life to the desolate wartime atmosphere and looking for companionship for Frances, famously offered the use of the Peacock Point squash court to Stacey as a weekend cottage. Stacey accepted the generous offer and set about making the squash court a home. Once again, bucolic Peacock Point found itself on the cutting edge of design. Blithe in spirit, Stacey's country house was the smash hit of unconventional design in the war years, making such a successful virtue of the wartime credo "make it do, or do without" that the house—if it could even be called that—remained his weekend retreat, virtually unaltered, for the next fifty years.

Capturing the spirit of the times and daringly imaginative, the squash court inevitably graced the cover of *House & Garden*. Fine eighteenth-century furniture lived with incongruous but stylish ease against the enameled white walls. A gilded chandelier hung from the ceiling. But lighthearted and casual touches relieved what could have been a forced formality. Geraniums in humble terra-cotta pots were scattered among crystal candelabras. It showed the world, once and forever, how taste and style transcended circumstance, pointing the way to the new less formal trends in postwar design, including an equally inventive country house that Stacey would have in France.

Living in a squash court demanded a certain raffish facility. For starters, entering the court through its low players' door required physical agility. Further, Mrs. Davison stipulated that Stacey could use the squash court for life (which he did, controversially), provided he not alter the athletic character of the space, so the bright enameled white board walls and red playing lines were elements to be worked around in a design scheme. (Fortunately, Stacey was increasingly drawn to a red and green palette.) The observation balcony became the bedroom. The mischievous Billy Baldwin recalls the squash-court-turned-cottage (somewhat inaccurately in regards to bathing facilities) as "an enchanting little house....A weekend there with him could not have [been] more fun. The bathroom facilities were slightly odd in that the shower was outside in front of the house; consequently, you had the advantage

After a stint with the Coast Guard and a WPA course in camouflage, Stacey closed his office and entered the Army as a first lieutenant. Given his skill with color and draftsmanship, Stacey was naturally assigned to the camouflage office. All went well as long as Stacey's work depended solely on technical skills; a new promotion required leadership skills, stirring up deep-rooted insecurities.

House & Garden

A Condé Nast Publication

Decoration Undated

2 Prize Houses

Ernest Walker
September 1945
Price 35 Cents   40 Cents in Canada

there of showing off to everybody." Part of the fun, Baldwin added, stemmed from the fact that the host mixed marvelous martinis.

Reestablishing his life in town, Stacey leased an apartment at 66 East 56th Street, which he filled with antiques accumulated over twenty years. His eye for composition, color, dramatic lighting, placement, and fine furniture produced results that *House & Garden* described as "timeless and distinguished, very often brilliant, with undefinable chic....a color sense of Renaissance braggadocio" and deep comfort as well. Reminiscent of the work of William Odom, gilt wood and mirrors sparkled against walls of deepwater green, while the matching carpet provided "an opulent depth." Stacey paired green with rose—the increasingly favored color scheme—adding curtains of a deep rose and upholstering Louis XVI chairs with a softer shade of rose. Tall candles in gilded sconces, brass banding on the Louis XV desk, mirrors, perfume burners, overscaled caryatid lamps, an ormolu clock, and a gilded carved console added bright notes to the space. Architectural drawings, landscape sketches, bas-relief panels, and personal mementos were artfully framed and hung with Stacey's usual flair for wall composition. What *House & Garden* cites as an "unbelievable, unhistorical mélange—Chinese, Louis XVI, Empire, Victorian" included a Japanese low table, a Boulle side table, classical urns, and a painted Italian screen. In a fainthearted design moment, the apartment was a beacon of style.

While life unfolded against the canvas of wartime, it nevertheless followed time-honored patterns. Café Society had long departed for war, but El Morocco and the Stork Club continued operations, often providing happy venues for wartime leaves. When Brenda Diana Duff Frazier, then Mrs. John "Shipwreck" Kelly, the original celebutante (the press coined the word for her in 1939), gave birth to a daughter in 1945, John Perona, owner of El Morocco, ended a congratulatory cable to his prize client with a sly reference to his competitor: "Please stop giving the Stork free publicity!" War or no war, the natural rhythm of life continued in whatever fashion it could muster. Thus, it followed that a new baby necessitated a new house for Brenda Frazier and her family, and, but of course, George Stacey would be hired to design it.

A devotee of romantic beds and Victoriana, Stacey combined both predilections in his acquisition of Queen Victoria's bed (opposite). He improvised bed curtains from damask tablecloths that he dyed green.

Architectural drawings, landscape sketches, bas-relief panels, and personal mementos were arranged by Stacey with an eye for balance and symmetry (above). The two arched frames hovering above the console contained sentimental memorabilia, including a hotel receipt bearing the names Mr. Stacey and Mr. Pahlmann. Stacey's hallmark, a penchant for classical forms, is well represented by a bust on a pedestal, urns, and decorative pediment figures.

Even in wartime, a Stacey room was destined for elegance. *Noting that wartime entertainment typically consisted of quiet gatherings of friends, Vogue featured what were then considered simple at-home evening dresses—photographed in the apartment of Mr. and Mrs. Edward Elkins—in an article entitled "Dinner with the Curtains Drawn." The apartment designed by Stacey featured a fantastical secretary with Chippendale-inspired pediment, a Louis XVI bergère, and an overscaled print on windows. Furniture profiles popped with razor-sharp precision against the dark walls. Stacey stalwarts, glittering sconces, supplied the finishing touch. Most would probably approve of the dinner-jacketed accessories, too.*

CHAPTER EIGHT

THE NEW LOOK

1945–1950

Stacey's country house, improbably situated in a squash court (opposite), was the smash hit of unconventional design in the war years. Mixing geraniums in humble pots, crystal candelabra, French furniture, and red playing lines, it pointed to the less formal trends of postwar design. Stacey's own rendering of the squash court (above) depicts a chauffeuse and fanciful tôle pagodas rakishly cohabiting with a casually draped chair.

Houseguest Billy Baldwin recalls the squash-court-turned-cottage as an enchanting little house with eccentric bathing facilities and marvelous martinis.

Representing a dramatic departure from the prevailing wartime aesthetic, Stacey's luxurious apartment at 66 East 56th Street showcased scale, composition, symmetry, dramatic lighting, and sensuous color. Noting the "unbelievable, unhistorical mélange of Chinese, Louis XVI, Empire, Victorian furniture with palace fabrics" and lots and lots of accessories, both big and small, the more personal the better, House & Garden summed up the apartment as "timeless and distinguished, very often brilliant, with undefinable chic."

A palette deemed "Renaissance braggadocio" by House & Garden included gilt wood, crystal, and mirrors sparkling against a background of deepwater green walls and rug, punctuated by the addition of bois de rose Louis XVI chairs and dark rose curtains. Symmetry and sharp profiles cut the richness with precision and pizzazz.

As the New Look burst upon the scene, extravagantly frothing yards and yards of newly available fabric, Stacey enjoyed a heady moment. His client list so glittered by now with glamour girls and power brokers that Billy Baldwin—newly arrived in New York—viewed Stacey as the reigning king of design. But even from his high perch in the design firmament, surrounded by Babe Paley, Brenda Frazier, and Diana Vreeland, Stacey's artistic antennae were picking up signals of change that translated into his designs. Just as the supple bias-cut dress of the 1930s had been replaced by the efficient broad-shouldered suit of the 1940s, now the artfully constructed ball gown became emblematic of postwar sensibility. Aligning with that new sensibility, Stacey's work—which had always had a baroque side to it—became mannered.

It was not without reason that *House & Garden* described Stacey as a "decorator, stage-set designer, and psychologist." Stacey invariably operated as a sort of aesthetic filter, parlaying contemporary moods and influences into au courant rooms. Now romance and illusion seduced a world caught in

the aftershock of war. For the clientele who snapped up gorgeous Dior dresses with escapist Belle Époque profiles, waspy waists, and billowing skirts, Stacey fashioned the interior design equivalent of the New Look: havens of make-believe, feverish color, and studied perfection. The creative spirit that thrived on experimentation—in the past producing shocking pink ceilings, stringy bed canopies, and dining rooms recast as supper clubs—delved into the new idiom, devised unusual color palettes, and occasionally relinquished the cool formalism that had characterized his earlier work.

The swagger of Somerset House in Paget Parish, Bermuda, signaled the arrival of a new era. Inspired by the eighteenth-century architecture, Stacey switched on his talents for color, scale, and placement with the flair of a showman for Frances and Frederick Wierdsma. In the Georgian tradition, the house is imposing, spare, and blocky; Stacey keyed these features right into the decoration, using clean sculptural outlines evocative of the facade, and then packed a few of his own punches. The underpinnings of the living room look familiar. Bittersweet chocolate walls and white architectural trim highlight the splendid tray ceiling; deep greens and clear reds charge a disciplined palette; white simple linen curtains, painted gothic crown molding, busts of Roman consuls, clock cases, and chair frames create assertive silhouettes against the brown walls. With a few sleights of hand, Stacey upturned conventions of scale: an enormous Federal mirror over the sofa dwarfs the seating area; it is balanced by another overscaled circle—a railway clock, irreverently whitewashed and carved with ribbons—hung over a square fireplace on the opposite side of the room. Much of the seating came from the dealer Frederick P. Victoria, whose career blossomed with the reopening of trade with Europe after World War II. Underfoot, Stacey placed a deep green carpet; for the upholstery, he used a bold, savvy chintz—barely related to the delicate florals that graced Mrs. Townsend Martin's house—that even Dorothy Draper, then transforming the Greenbrier from military hospital to resort hotel with her signature cabbage rose chintz, would have admired. It is the intelligent, assured work of a master done for a worldly-wise client.

With the same sure hand operating on a more subtle scale, Stacey created a new paneled drawing room overlooking Fifth Avenue for Frances and Ward Cheney. A sophisticated palette—honey and toned aqua splashed

A fter years of restraint and anxiety, it was time for fantasy. Christian Dior captured the shift in mood with his ebullient New Look, while Stacey responded similarly with mannered interiors.

with apricot and lemon—now appeared and brought with it the expected Stacey twist: brilliant citron yellow accents inject astringency into an otherwise calm room. More painted pieces begin to appear—an Italian bombé commode and a graceful chair—and they accentuate shape and profile in the overall composition, while the reupholstered *borne*, the Italian gilt-wood bench, and the famous string rug from the prewar duplex make repeat appearances. And while it seems superfluous to mention the usual elements—bronze-and-gilt candelabra, traces of gilt bronze, crystal, and gilt wood that add the gleam and reflective qualities requisite to Stacey's aesthetic—a large Régence mirror and Baltic chandelier (that appears romantically lit solely by candles) are notable shiny new additions. Typical of Stacey, too, are the understated curtains.

Upstairs from the Cheney apartment at 4 East 66th Street lived Mr. and Mrs. Philip Isles and their children. Lil Isles, a much-photographed darling of *Vogue* editors and another dream of a client, ushered

The eighteenth-century Somerset House in Paget Parish, Bermuda (below), signaled Stacey's new point of view. Taking his cues from the sharp-cut Georgian architecture, Stacey imprinted the interiors with an authoritative flourish.

Dwarfing a sofa with an enormous Federal mirror and dominating a mantel with a railway clock, Stacey upturned known conventions of scale in the Somerset House living room (overleaf). Espresso walls calmed the exuberant chintz (a distant relative to the delicate florals in the Townsend Martin house, but close kin to the cabbage roses employed by Dorothy Draper then transforming the Greenbrier from a military hospital to a resort) and drew attention to the Gothic cornice and classical busts. Additional strokes of white, including a Bermuda tray ceiling and a neoclassical lamp, provide snap and sass.

A sophisticated palette of honey and toned aqua appears in an elegant new living room for Frances and Ward Cheney, with citron accents adding youthful zest. Beguiling the eye with lively profiles, an Italian bombé commode and a graceful chair signal the increasing importance of painted pieces in Stacey's aesthetic. Ever the Yankee, Stacey reused the Italian gilt-wood bench, center borne, and famous string rug from the Cheneys' prewar duplex.

into Stacey's oeuvre an entirely new sensibility. As a dedicated painter—her children remember her painting every weekend in the country—Lil Isles was not one to shy away from color. Like Frances Cheney, she was also something of an iconoclast—when she skied in St. Moritz without makeup (!) the news rippled through the pages of *Vogue*. With her self-assured taste, Mrs. Isles provided Stacey with two empty canvases—in town and on Long Island—to explore new ideas, engendering results that were smart, innovative, and much admired among the stylish set. Many of its members recall with awe both the country house and apartment much as they do Lil Isles herself: "breathtakingly attractive—the *most* chic." However, these homes were not for the faint of heart.

In fact, the Isles dining room in town was so spare, stylized, and eclectic that it was nearly intimidating—at least for the children, who remember the endlessly long table commissioned from Frederick P. Victoria (today, Frederick P. Victoria and Son still makes the Isles table) and imposing high-backed chairs as something from the addled tea party in *Alice in Wonderland*. (Philip Isles, a partner at Lehman Brothers, must have been amused to find himself with a high-style dining room that contrasted so greatly with the legendarily clubby Lehman partners' dining room.) Stacey filled the room with arch surprises, updating eighteenth-century furniture, painting baroque chairs a chalky white, silhouetting their shaped crimson backs against turquoise walls, and laying understated solid carpeting. Accessories worthy of Ali Baba—or Rose Cumming—finished the room: a Chinese verre églomisé screen, an attenuated tôle chandelier, a gilded console, and a commanding Queen Anne mirror. The Isles were renowned for their art collection, so it is notable that Stacey did not feel the need to hang any paintings in this room. With, as *House & Garden* described it, a palette of "colors from an Italian painting in a New York dining room," perhaps paintings were considered redundant.

Equally sophisticated and very adult—it was off-limits to children—was the shimmering all-white, mirrored sitting room, while the grand living room overlooking Fifth Avenue, designed around an enormous painting dominating one wall, was elegantly treated with gray walls, silvery satin, and aubergine silk. Children were largely kept out of the way in those days, but the Isles children remember Stacey as a some-

L il Isles (above), a much-photographed darling of Vogue, was a self-assured iconoclast—when she appeared in St. Moritz without makeup (!), the news rippled through the pages of Vogue. For Isles, Stacey created daring, color-infused houses much admired among the stylish set. In the words of Gloria Schiff, the country house was "breathtakingly attractive—the most chic—and unlike any other house."

The Isles' dining room in town (opposite) was so spare, stylized, and eclectic that it was nearly intimidating—at least for the children, who remember an endlessly long table and imposing high-backed chairs worthy of Alice in Wonderland's addled tea party. Stacey filled the room with arch surprises and injected exotic accessories worthy of Ali Baba—or Rose Cumming.

what dapper yet forbidding presence (in fact, he was as painfully shy with children as he was with adults) who nevertheless created one room that earned their complete approval: a guest bedroom with flower-garlanded beds that one daughter desperately coveted for her own bedroom. With its pristine blanket covers and bed linens, the room at first glance conveys a demure quality, but the string carpet impishly contrasts with the Louis XV–inspired furniture, while the (discarded) victory wreaths on the bedposts inject wry humor into the decorum.

On weekends, the Isles family's country house on the North Shore of Long Island filled with guests from town, who exclaimed over its sensational design. Whereas the city apartment was cerebral and studied, the country house fairly exploded with life. Stacey's color scheme was unabashed: walls were a shocking fresh white at a time when toned colors were in vogue, each room differentiated by vivid color—lavender, green, and red clashing with vibrant pink. Majolica porcelain fruit rested everywhere; paintings, many by Lil and Philip Isles, others by renowned artists, filled the walls. The children admired the city apartment at a respectful distance, but they adored their Stacey country house with its sun porch full of comfortable bamboo furniture, sitting rooms with deep down-filled sofas and chairs, and lively color throughout. And while other designs of the postwar era feel deliberate and careful, the Isles country house was refreshing in its gaiety.

While design historians lament the transience of interior design, subject to inevitable deterioration in the course of time as well as life changes of the owners, the remnants of Stacey's designs for the North Shore home came to a particularly dramatic end. As the family began to spend less time in Sands Point, the

*T*he Isles children remember Stacey as a somewhat dapper yet *forbidding presence (in fact, he was as painfully shy with children as he was with adults) who nevertheless created one room that earned their complete approval: a guest bedroom with flower-garlanded beds that one daughter desperately coveted for her own bedroom. Though the pristine blanket covers and bed linens convey all the ladylike decorum of the New Look, the (discarded) victory wreaths on the bedposts inject wry humor into respectability.*

house was rented to a string of musicians, ending with Keith Richards of the Rolling Stones, accompanied by actress/model/sorceress Anita Pallenberg, infamous for incidents of throwing bottles of red wine when in need of a heroin fix. Pallenberg apparently experienced many such crises in Sands Point, for an Isles son reports they returned to a ravaged house—coincidentally littered with mysterious traces of witchcraft: plastic domes, animal carcasses, and white powder.

Not far away from the North Shore of Long Island, Lil Isles's fellow *Vogue* model, the new Mrs. William Paley, hired her old decorator Stacey to create a rarefied environment at Kiluna Farm. William Paley, running a CBS television empire that would define communication in the twentieth century, had purchased the nineteenth-century property with his first wife in the 1930s; a visitor noted that "it was polite and pretty, rather like a nice country club"—so it was clearly ready for the fashionable imprint of the new Mrs. Paley. As Mrs. Stanley Mortimer, Babe had once scoured antique stores on Third Avenue with Stacey for treasures at relatively modest prices; now as the wife of William Paley, a titan who took matters of style and design very seriously (his gold World War II dog tag was custom-made at Cartier), all design objects and objectives were attainable. Of course, there was no conceivable reason why a low-ceilinged white clapboard house could not be transformed into a Belle Époque country house.

Never again would Kiluna Farm be a conventional American home; instead, it would be refined, exquisite, and studied. Babe, the ardent Francophile—who had had a taste for anything Louis XIV, XV, or XVI instilled in her by Stacey—was now antiquing in Paris with Stacey by her side. (Coincidentally, French furniture had by this time become once again a "must" for the fashionable set.) A photo shows the two on their rounds of *antiquaires*, Babe holding spotless gloves and peering intently into a window; Stacey, upright and in the role of tutor, wearing sunglasses and his characteristic hat; Paris seductive and still around them (see page 6).

After antiquing, they would adjourn to Stacey's new apartment in Paris—which was conveniently close to the great Left Bank dealers—to smoke, review their finds, and make final selections to ship to New York. Finally, Babe, clad in a dress by Charles James, was able to pose for *Vogue*'s camera in her Proustian living room. The gorgeous dress, in Titian red with a nineteenth-century

B abe Paley, in a Titian-red dress with nineteenth-century silhouette by Charles James poses in her Proustian living room (opposite). Stacey conjured the spirit of the Belle Époque by placing downy pillows on a deeply tufted sofa, packing hothouse leaves into porcelain de Paris cachepots, and assembling an eclectic collection of French furniture to showcase William Paley's French nineteenth-century paintings. The aura of dense comfort is intensified by a nervous palette of aqua, sulphuric green, and bois de rose keyed to the Matisse, Rousseau, Toulouse-Lautrec, and Cézanne paintings.

Paley and Stacey review a day's worth of antiques in Stacey's Paris apartment (above), bonding over their shared passion for antiquing. Stacey invested Babe with his eye for French furniture. Despite a few decorative additions, including the superb urn of tôle lilies on bracket, the rue de la Chaise apartment retained the elegant austerity remembered by Charles Sevigny.

Ardent Francophile
Babe Paley filled
her bedroom at Kiluna
Farm almost entirely with
French pieces. Under Stacey's
tutelage, she also seemingly
developed a weakness for
blackamoors. The tufted
upholstery, black lacquer
desk, and chalky Louis XV
chairs exhibit the postwar
Stacey touch. Generally,
Stacey, like William Odom,
preferred solid-colored
rugs and simple window
treatments in accordance with
French taste. In this room, he
made an exception, furthering
the Proustian idiom with
crenellated window valances
and patterned carpeting.

*S*tacey's designs in the 1940s were increasingly distinguished by a signature use of red and green, a palette suited to debutante-of-the-century Brenda Diana Duff Frazier (opposite), "the most glamorous, black-haired, gardenia-skinned, ruby-lipped debutante who ever wore a strapless dress," according to The New York Times. For Frazier, who had set the fashion for red lipstick, Stacey worked vivid notes of crimson into a living room in Oyster Bay, New York. The dining room (above) explored the range of green.

While the great London florist Constance Spry designed the flowers for Brenda Frazier's debut, Stacey, a master of contrast, advocated loose unstudied garden flowers to offset the cool perfection of both Brenda Frazier and his decorous designs for the debutante.

silhouette, might well have been chosen for its perfect accord with the room, which includes a Toulouse-Lautrec painting hanging over an impressively carved Louis XV console. Stacey draped the deeply tufted sofa with downy pillows, packed hothouse leaves into porcelain de Paris cachepots, and hung Bill Paley's paintings by Henri Matisse, Henri Rousseau, and Paul Cézanne to create an aura of dense comfort offset by a tense palette of aqua, sulphuric green, and faded rose keyed to the paintings.

A French boudoir with low ceilings, broad windows, and simple architectural trim is an incongruous proposition, but Stacey's eclectic, inviting, and highly personal bedroom for Babe Paley managed its own cozy aesthetic. Like Babe in her most elegant turnouts, the spacious, light room retained an appealing American niceness. Stacey inserted his customary components of chalky Louis XV chairs, a blackamoor, a *bibliothèque*, tufted upholstery, and lacquer while venturing into nineteenth-century territory with a palette of greens and ivory en camaïeu, floral-pattern carpeting and crenellated window valances that recalled Viollet-le-Duc—all far removed from the simple backgrounds Stacey usually employed in his rooms.

If life at Kiluna Farm seemed a little contrived, debutante of the century Brenda Diana Duff Frazier—"the most glamorous, black-haired, gardenia-skinned, ruby-lipped debutante who ever wore a strapless dress" (and by this time Mrs. John Simms Kelly)—appeared so artificial that it was rumored she based her highly distinctive personal style on an inhuman model: Disney's Snow White, who had made her own smashing debut the year before Brenda. Despite inordinate press attention (what we would call "overexposure" today), Brenda Frazier had somehow remained sweet, generous, and fundamentally tentative, making her very careful to get everything just right. And if you were a hesitant twenty-seven-year-old society matron who had just acquired Meadow Wood Farm in Oyster Bay, it was a given that Stacey, as the ruling society decorator, should be called in for the decoration. For this careful, highly polished princess, Stacey designed a set piece of perfection.

Although the brick Georgian house was relatively new, Stacey invested it with a sense of timelessness, filling it with flowers and pretty colors while tucking in his smart Venetian mirrors, blackamoors, and lacquer. Brenda loved the results so much that as her

life wandered from Oyster Bay to Park Avenue and then on to Cape Cod and Boston, she trailed with her the glamorous post-debutante trappings George had amassed for her, updating him with notes and photos over the years. *Vogue*, too, admired the coolly refined house and noted its illusory qualities, commenting that the manor house gave the outward appearance of having been lived in a long time and bore the look of "a plot of Virginia moved north."

Dramatic yet serene, with references to Frazier's demure, ladylike style, Meadow Wood Farm personifies Brenda Frazier as channeled by Stacey. She looks fabulous in her house, prompting the consideration that her frequently copied red lipstick may have had much to do with the honing of Stacey's signature red and green palette—the artfully groomed faces that women wore in those decades came alive against those colors. Seated in her George Stacey drawing room, Frazier gazes at the camera, lovely and poised against her new paneled walls, pearls wrapped multiple times around her wrist and throat (after all, Babe Paley and Diana Vreeland did that, so it must be fashionable), opaline glass echoing an emerald bracelet clasp, and pomegranate pillows contrasting with celadon damask upholstery. A Venetian mirror and tiered mahogany tables, all of which earned places in Frazier's homes for the rest of her life, balance her damask sofa. A tiny chair inlaid with mother-of-pearl, similar to one Stacey placed in Frances Cheney's boudoir, keeps the requisite finishing touch of black in play, a reminder of the far-off easy chic preached in a prewar "Why Don't You…" column.

Across the room, saturated Stacey jewel tones—a rosy Marshall Field–style sofa, lush bottle green carpeting, Chippendale chairs with daffodil-colored seats—glow against the pine paneled walls (see page 5). Whereas accessories were often used sparingly in Stacey rooms (with an exception made for the exuberant Diana Vreeland), Stacey indulged his love of arranging *objets* in the Kellys' home. Jade, cachepots, export porcelain—rabbits, fancifully—and paintings cover the table, mantel, and wall surfaces. Stacey also had influence on the flowers, favoring an offhand approach. For the girl who had London's celebrated florist Constance Spry provide the flowers for her debutante party, Stacey dictated masses of flowers, not "arrangements," but simple country flowers—snapdragons and rhododendrons—that offset the pervasive perfection with a note of nonchalance.

Of course, Brenda Frazier entertained perfectly. Her guests included the Duke and Duchess of Windsor and her neighbors C. Z. and Winston Guest, mixed with friends from the El Morocco/Stork Club circuit, such as Bing Crosby and Count Vava Alderberg, a protégé of Prince Serge Obolensky. And the hostess sparkled as brightly as her guest list with her perfect hair, a freshly polished red manicure, and a prominent display of silver. The site of her many dinner parties was Stacey's monochromatic Georgian dining room en camaïeu vert, where Frazier's collection of green Rockingham porcelain was displayed in fluted-shell niches. Amid the emerald, forest, and bottle greens in the neoclassical setting, Stacey placed a glittering crystal chandelier, girandoles, and a striking black Coromandel screen. In the more modern white and green breakfast room,

---

M rs. Anthony Drexel Duke poses expectantly for Vogue in a schoolgirlish white blouse and grown-up red lipstick. *Against innovative chalky white walls, Stacey placed a Venetian mirror, a carved French console, Louis XV chairs, and an imposingly tall Coromandel screen—his frequent trick for achieving scale and worldliness. While the antiques and palette lend an Old World formality to the space, Stacey also airlifted a few traces of modernity into the room: wall-to-wall carpet (a postwar innovation) and the splayed-leg wood table showing influences of Edward Wormley in the foreground. The clear reds and greens used for Somerset House in Bermuda and Brenda Frazier in Oyster Bay shift to a sharp palette of El Greco colors: cardinal red silk curtains, accents of moss and mustard satin.*

---

a clever inversion of the dining room scheme, Stacey gathered more of those prized black and gold accents—a black lacquer commode, blackamoors (by now Vreeland and Stacey had made them indispensable), and Chinese lacquer bowls.

Other young women sought grown-up interiors, too, for sophistication seems to have been desirable then. Mrs. Anthony Drexel Duke poses expectantly for *Vogue* in a schoolgirlish white blouse and grown-up red lipstick in *her* George Stacey–designed living room. While the antiques and palette lent an Old World formality to the space, Stacey airlifted a few traces of modernity into the room: wall-to-wall carpet, a postwar trend, appears, as

When Town & Country *published the Cheneys' country house (right) for the second time in 1949, the living room had acquired its own New Look. With the introduction of a half dozen small-scale upholstered chairs, it was now curvy and sociable. Flowers, books, potpourri, cards, and even a few flounced skirts transformed the formerly dramatic stage-set drawing room into an inviting country living room.

A six-panel Chinese screen sheltering a Louis XV writing table carved out a sophisticated corner (overleaf left) in the Cheneys' living room. The moody rendering by John C. Hulse shows that the room retained its original pale chocolate-colored walls.

At the fireplace (overleaf right), a mirror duplicated on the opposite wall provides an endless succession of views of the chandelier for a dramatic evening focus. The cascades of wood drapery, now coupled with paintings by de Chirico, show Stacey in full command of his wall composition skills, while a towering bookcase and diminutive bergères register scale. A leitmotif of green—the lacquer bookcase, the emerald rug, and the turquoise footstool—laced the cocoa-colored room with continuity.

it does in other rooms of this era. Stacey the innovator emerges briefly to place a splayed-leg wood table showing influences of Edward Wormley in the foreground. (It was about this time that William Pahlmann and Stacey were friendly, and their reciprocal influence shows up in both designers' work.) With innovative chalky white walls, Stacey layered a Venetian mirror as well as a mirrored-top coffee table, a carved French console, Louis XV chairs, neoclassical urn lamps, and an imposingly tall Coromandel screen—his frequent trick for achieving scale and worldliness. Again, Stacey experimented with unusual color tonalities. The clear reds and greens used for the Wierdsmas' house in Bermuda and Brenda Frazier's in Oyster Bay shift to a sharp palette of El Greco colors: cardinal red silk curtains and accents of moss and mustard satin.

Judging by the changes in her country house, even Frances Cheney was altered by the war. When *Town & Country* published the house for the second time, in February 1949, it revealed a house significantly transformed. Postwar living, social structures, unavailability of staff, and a faster pace were reshaping American lifestyles. The former spare elegance of the great room had become warm and informal. Many of the chic old elements were still apparent, such as the wood swags flanking the mantel and the custom Greek-key bookcase behind the curved sofa. A half dozen small-scale upholstered chairs—in a style that to this day is sometimes called a "Stacey chair" by old-time custom upholsterers in New York City—were added to the space, promoting comfort and conversation; two are covered in an atypical printed cotton and have ruffled skirts. Books, flowers, potpourri, cards, and ashtrays further transformed the formerly dramatic stage-set drawing room into an inviting country living room.

Minnie Astor, too, was ready for change, and Stacey obliged with an urban interpretation of Somerset House in Bermuda, a stylish exercise in profile, scale, and deep cornflower blue. Using Minnie's favorite shade of blue, Stacey painted the room from baseboards to crown molding, exaggerating the loftiness of an already tall room. Offsetting the intensity of color, Stacey designed white curtains with a smartly outlined baroque-shaped cornice. He added a Louis XV white marble mantel, a white-ground chintz, and a curiously small pair of porcelain horses on the mantel, while a Venetian mirror, beaded crystal sconces, and shiny satin contributed

S tacey outfitted the back wall of the dining porch at Peacock Point (above) with mirrors to reflect Long Island Sound—a blessing for diners with their backs to the water. Table and chairs by Drouet sporting pink cushions and a painted screen of a bird's-eye view of Peacock Point fulfill the requirements for alfresco panache.

For the blue-eyed Minnie Astor, Stacey repainted the living room cornflower blue (opposite). The room was one in a long line that garnered Stacey's reputation as "the jewel man." Decorating for the three Cushing sisters—New York's reigning glamour girls—prompted Billy Baldwin to describe Stacey as the "king of decorators."

the shimmer that was Stacey's wont. Stacey the colorist added accents of garnet in the fireplace benches and emerald satin on club chairs for full jewel-box effect.

For someone Billy Baldwin saw as a king among decorators, Stacey kept a rather low profile. Of course, he had his share of publicity, and he was quoted and noted in magazines and newspapers. He also adored the attentions of the glamorous, independent, and witty style setters who were the mainstay of his business. But due to his shyness, he was never given to grand socializing or fashionable industry camarade-

rie; more often, he was content to drop in casually on colleagues for easy sessions of gossip and updates. As his ties with Eleanor Brown, Ethel Smith, and Grace Fakes dated back to the 1920s and were associated with happy memories of design school, William Odom, and Paris, he was particularly prone to saunter over to McMillen, on nearby East 55th Street. However, he was also known to make unannounced visits to his design pals at Ruby Ross Wood and Thedlow, where he would eccentrically wear his hat indoors to mask the premature baldness that so upset him.

As a former antique dealer, Stacey forever enjoyed talking shop with other dealers, and he became particularly close to Frederick P. Victoria, who not only was known for an unusual French and Italian inventory that resonated with Stacey's baroque sympathies, but also produced smart custom furniture that made its way into many Stacey rooms. Over the years, a kind of weekly dinner ritual evolved. Stacey shared a cocktail with Mrs. Victoria then dined with the family while glowering like a headmaster at the two mischievous young sons.

Although Stacey was warmly welcomed by his friends at McMillen and every antique dealer in town, his prickly personality drew detractors, too. Artist Jeremiah Goodman, who had worked with him for a *House & Garden* story in the 1940s, compares Stacey to Cecil Beaton, recalling both as "insecure, pompous and rude, and not *exactly* attractive." Maybe the handsome young Jeremiah was just a shade *too* gorgeous for the defensive, prematurely bald Stacey, for although touchy, he could be kind. Perhaps remembering the critical difference a timely assist could make in forging a career, he made time to meet Albert Hadley when the young veteran was exploring the possibility of moving to New York and thoughtfully paved the way for Hadley to have an interview with Eleanor Brown at McMillen. (When Hadley arrived at Stacey's apartment for their meeting, Stacey discreetly pretended to take a phone call in another room, giving his young visitor time to take in the apartment he had memorized from the *House & Garden* spread.)

On weekends, Stacey made ample use of the squash court at Peacock Point, where life fell back into the old familiar rhythms of croquet with assorted Davisons, Cheneys, Gates, and Guinzburgs and visiting with Mrs. Davison. He and Frances Cheney continued their close friendship. But the charming Helen Marshall was still his special friend, and their friendship was buoyed by new proximity. In 1946, after the war ended, Helen and Hannath Marshall moved to New York, where the debonair Hannath eventually wrote copy at Ogilvy and Helen painted, networked in the New York art world, and taught life drawing at Parsons School of Design. Per Stanley Barrows of Parsons, Helen Marshall was a fabulous teacher, one of the best ever for life drawing. Given Stacey's wartime encounter with his own limitations as a communicator, Helen's gift for teaching, drawing on confidence and easy interaction, as well as expertise, was yet another quality for George to admire.

William Pahlmann, the archetypal postwar decorator, ushered hi-fi consoles, rec rooms, and far-flung artifacts into the decorating mainstream. The friendship between Stacey and Pahlmann produced artistic crossovers: Stacey's work would develop a breezy streak in the upcoming decade, and William Pahlmann ventured into uncharacteristically formal terrain. Assembling a Coromandel screen, Louis XVI chair, mirrored coffee table, neoclassical terne lamp, passementerie-based cigarette table and unified palette for Walter Hoving, Pahlmann channeled Stacey hallmarks into an elegant living room (opposite).

In turn, Stacey's fascination with alternative dining rooms produced a smoky-walled haven with a cherry red rug (below), a table seating ten, and low-slung "tous les Louis" Palmann-esque slipper chairs recorded in Vogue's "Decorators' Notes" column.

CHAPTER NINE

FRENCH CONNECTIONS

1950–1960

As Stacey approached fifty, the stars aligned to draw him back to Paris: the antique dealer Jean-Louis Raynaud offered him an available apartment in the ever-desirable Faubourg Saint-Germain. Stacey's successful practice allowed him the freedom to come and go at will, and Paris, always compelling, was particularly welcoming to Americans after the war. It seems, too, that the decorating gods had conspired with a purpose, for returning to Paris brought Stacey full circle as a designer. The reconnection with French architecture reaffirmed his roots as a classicist, banishing the mannered tendencies that had cropped up in his work in the 1940s. Stacey's natural reductive style returned, and he produced designs that were balanced and poised while still retaining a tantalizing hint of the baroque. The red and green palette clarified; at times it even ceded to new, gorgeous colors. Ever the filter for social trends, Stacey now created rooms with a distinctive American breeziness, reflecting the shift from high-maintenance, studied perfection to more contemporary, streamlined living. The diamond-sharp

gems he produced for Leon and Blanche Levy, Grace Kelly, and himself were worthy of Tiffany settings.

The idyllic pattern of spending more time in Paris began in an apartment in an aristocratic townhouse at 1, rue de la Chaise. The new apartment benefited from a prime location on the piano nobile, providing Stacey with the high ceilings and classic proportions expected of aristocratic reception rooms prior to the French Revolution. Fortunately, too, the former inhabitants—the Comte de Vertus and members of the Bethune-Polignac family—had given the house fashionable face-lifts in the eighteenth century, leaving a legacy of tall French windows, paneled walls, and parquet de Versailles floors. As his aesthetic increasingly reaffirmed its neoclassical roots, Stacey assembled a collection of Louis XVI and Directoire furniture that recalled the strict aesthetic of William Odom, though he added his own signatures of brilliant color, austere white walls, and gilded accessories, including gilt-wood fragments that glinted from atop the bookcase. The result was a cool essay on modern classicism.

In Paris as in New York, Stacey was a notable personage. International designer Charles Sevigny, then a very young man, remembers being brought to meet Stacey by Van Day Truex, then director of the Parsons School of Design. While the elder men chatted, probably about the Parsons curriculum, the observant Sevigny noted the interiors of the master. He was seeing the apartment under interesting circumstances. There were as yet no accessories in place, no rug, only the eighteenth-century furniture still upholstered in white muslin—evidently Stacey had just moved in—but sixty years later, Sevigny could still recall the exquisite beauty of the apartment and the fine caliber of the antiques. Without the color so characteristic of Stacey's work, the aristocratic spare space projected an atypical Miss Havisham–like beauty, one that Van Day Truex, an ardent proponent of no-color interiors, would surely have sanctioned. And though Truex and Stacey had very different color sensibilities and styles, they shared a mutual respect for classicism, as well as each other's professionalism. Truex had asked Stacey to serve as an adviser at Parsons, which, sadly for both design students and Stacey, was a short-lived arrangement due to Stacey's touchy nature. Basically, he seems to have resigned over some minor bureaucratic issue. Always his own worst enemy, Stacey was plagued by insecurity that often flared around the handsome, sociable Truex, a situation that Billy Baldwin attributed to a kind of schoolboy rivalry between two brilliant students who had both been worthy of William Odom's attention.

When back in the States, Stacey had his usual stylish clients to keep him busy. Blanche Levy, Bill Paley's sister, commissioned Stacey to decorate a Palm Beach house that radiated the new smartness. Whereas Paley's own Kiluna Farm was an exercise in esoteric, high-strung style, his sister's house was even-tempered and collected. Blanche Levy, who was known for her own impeccable style, had complete faith in Stacey. (Stacey had earned his stripes with Blanche Levy with an urbane design of Venetian mirrors, moss-fringed sofas, and Giacometti lamps for her neoclassical house in Philadelphia.) In great form, as always, when working with a confident client, Stacey produced a masterpiece in Palm Beach. A glistening black parquet de Versailles floor offset white walls and upholstery, and the whole

At 1, rue de la Chaise, Stacey assembled a collection of French neoclassical furniture that recalled the strict aesthetic of William Odom updated with brilliant color, austere white walls, and gilded accessories, including gilt-wood fragments glinting from atop the bookcase. The result was a cool essay on modern living in a historic space.

was brought to life with minimal touches of color. Fresh spring colors—clear emerald green, jonquil, and coral—were used sparingly and to great effect. The "palace fabrics" so typical of Stacey were now replaced with simple linens—crisp off-white linen for windows, off-white linen damask for upholstery.

Taking advantage of his new pied-à-terre in Paris and the postwar antique prices, Stacey purchased furniture and objects in Paris with a liberal hand, acquiring extraordinary pieces for the Levys. The Italian marble overdoor used in place of a mantel in the dining room reveals a stroke of particular creativity, while witty tôle trees add character to the living room. Dark objects, including the Coromandel screen, add drama, while fanciful tôle sconces, jardinieres with flamboyant fringe, and the inspired tassels on the table skirt keep the tone relaxed. Severe Chinese low tables, plain rugs, and

Stacey's interiors for Blanche and Leon Levy in Palm Beach radiated smartness while complementing the reductive classicism of architect John L. Volk.

The Levys' airy pavilion is a study in symmetry and pairs. A glistening black parquet de Versailles floor offset white walls (right, and overleaf, left), enclosing a furniture plan that quietly slipped antiques (pairs of Louis XVI chairs, demilune consoles, gilt-wood barometers, atheniennes, tôle trees, Chinese altars, and Italian lamps) amid modern furniture (pairs of sofas, coffee tables, étagères). The "palace fabrics" so typical of Stacey were now replaced by simple off-white linen. A Coromandel screen and a secretary at opposite ends of the room keep the sight lines high.

The joyous foil of spring green and jonquil against a Coromandel screen and ebonized floor brings charm to the Levy living room (overleaf, top right), while fanciful tassels on a table skirt and simple pots of bamboo update elegant Louis XVI furnishings, gilt-wood, ormolu, and opaline.

Taking advantage of his pied-à-terre in Paris and postwar antique bargains, Stacey astutely purchased antiques in Paris. An Italian marble overdoor ingeniously used as a mantel (overleaf, bottom right) and fanciful faux palm trees were trophies of transatlantic shopping. Notes of coral animate this sophisticated dining room.

I n the Levy study (above), Louis XVI and midcentury
furniture mingle harmoniously, while a magnificent framed
textile over the mantel adds oomph to a restful room.

    Repeated use of pairs and precise symmetry of tabletop
accessories create orderly calm in the Levy master bedroom
(opposite), while Stacey's adept weaving of tonal values ensures
that the spare, pale space retains visual interest. A Régence
mirror, dark marble console brackets, and a lacquer writing table
add strong focal points, while hand-painted Chinese wallpaper
panels dance the eye toward the tray ceiling.

At 988 Fifth Avenue, Stacey updated French style with a light touch for actress Grace Kelly (above). A shared sense of humor, love of things French, and lack of pretense forged an enduring bond between the two: Kelly would not only hire Stacey to update the palace at Monaco, but would also be a friend ever after.

With his mainstays of scale, strong profile, and contrast in firm control, Stacey succeeded Emilio Terry at the Palais Princier in Monaco. Working with the preexisting framework, Stacey emphasized architecture and underplayed fuss (opposite). Curtains sharply outlined with green taffeta, symmetrically placed chairs with dark green seats, and the strong central focus of a magnificently draped table under a chandelier make for a chic reception room. The deep green velvet table skirt—a rich triumph of embroidery and ribbon work—is suavely topped with a bold ceramic vase filled with sculptural rhododendron leaves.

abundant natural light highlight a collection of sculptural baroque and neoclassical antiques that Stacey had selected astutely for the Levys. While the fine Louis XVI pieces were unquestionably good investments, the more daring purchases also passed the test of time. Just as many of Frances Cheney's antiques are now found in the houses of successive generations, members of a third generation of Levys still derive pleasure from Stacey's singular eye. In fact, the tôle trees recently graced a granddaughter's wedding reception and now reside on a family horse farm in Kentucky, while other pieces continue to lend their smart aura to other family houses.

Over the years, Grace Kelly was in and out of the neighboring Levy house in Philadelphia, playing with the Levy children, which perhaps explains how the future princess first became aware of George Stacey. As she grew older, it was natural that she would seek out Stacey, for despite her all-American background, Grace displayed all the tendencies of a dedicated Francophile: like Babe Paley, she gravitated to fine French furniture; her favorite authors—Balzac and Montaigne—were French; and a favored squire was the French actor Jean-Pierre Aumont. In the early years of her film career, Grace Kelly lived in Skidmore, Owings and Merrill's Le Corbusier–inspired Manhattan House (for which her father had supplied the white brick) amidst cast-off family furniture, but after attaining success with *Mogambo*, *The Country Girl*, and *To Catch a Thief*, she moved on to something more to her own taste: an apartment with a living room, a library, and a dining room overlooking Central Park, four bedrooms, and one of the highest rents in town ($633.69 a month) at 988 Fifth Avenue. She looked to Stacey to design French-inflected interiors.

In the apartment, which overlooked the Metropolitan Museum of Art, George updated French style with a light touch for the actress. Like the red and green palette for Brenda Frazier, the ivory and pale blue used in the living room with eighteenth-century French antiques, stylish custom tables from Frederick P. Victoria, and abundant flowers, delivered twice weekly, seemed expressly designed to showcase Kelly. In addition to being beautiful, the design actually functioned for a contemporary, successful career woman, allowing the actress to hostess elegant dinner parties and informal gatherings alike. While Kelly was attending the Cannes Film Festival, her life famously changed course, causing her to abandon the lovely apartment, barely used. But a shared sense

GEORGE STACEY AND THE CREATION OF AMERICAN CHIC

of humor (his was droll, hers was playful), love of all things French, and down-to-earth lack of pretense had already forged a bond between Kelly and Stacey. Grace Kelly would not only remain a devoted client, but would also be a friend ever after. When Lee Radziwill, in the course of establishing a design career, proposed working with the princess on highly favorable terms for a project at Olympic Tower, Grace loyally responded that she couldn't possibly use any decorator other than her good friend George Stacey.

Not long after her April 1956 wedding, the new princess brought Stacey to Monte Carlo to spruce up the palace. This was a delicate task for a new bride—particularly as the groom had previously called in the services of Emilio Terry for the private apartments—but Princess Grace quickly found a diplomatic loophole: her pregnancy necessitated a nursery, which Stacey (whose style doesn't particularly dial up visions of children's rooms) gamely provided in Princess Grace's favorite color, yellow, and finished off with a Picasso print of a happy king.

Thereafter, with his mainstays of scale, strong profile, and contrast in firm control, Stacey designed a smartly turned-out reception room in ivory and magnolia green. Working with the preexisting architecture, which included a terrazzo floor and well-proportioned windows, Stacey emphasized the architecture and underplayed fuss, making a convincing case that less is more. Stacey sharply outlined white curtains with green taffeta and rosettes, placed four white-painted chairs with dark green seats symmetrically against the walls, and created a strong central focus with a magnificently draped table under the chandelier. The sumptuous deep green velvet table skirt—a rich triumph of embroidery and ribbon work by the famous *petites mains* of French tradition—was suavely topped with a bold ceramic vase filled with sculptural rhododendron leaves.

In all his work in Monaco, Stacey combined dignity with a modesty becoming to modern-day princes and princesses. For the Salon des Glaces, with its white and gold paneling and illusionistic ceiling, Stacey brought the same less-is-more approach that he used for the small reception room, discreetly adding yellow silk curtains with arched Empire pelmets (hanging with the luxurious drape of a good workroom behind them, of course) and refreshing the upholstery on the Directoire chairs. Minimal but bold strokes were also applied to the handsomely vaulted Salle des Gardes, where Stacey

In Monaco, Stacey combined dignity with a modesty becoming to modern-day princesses. For the Salon des Glaces (opposite) Stacey brought the same less-is-more approach that he used for the reception room, discreetly adding yellow silk curtains with arched Empire pelmets and refreshing upholstery on the Directoire chairs. Beyond Princess Caroline, the anteroom can be glimpsed through the French doors.

Minimal but bold strokes were just the thing for the handsomely vaulted Salle des Gardes (above), where Stacey painted the walls Prussian blue, hung Grimaldi armorial tapestries, and scattered various Oriental carpets on the floor for a continental interpretation of the "undecorated" look just emerging in the States.

painted the walls Prussian blue, hung Grimaldi armorial tapestries, and scattered various Oriental carpets on the floor for a dramatic interpretation of the "undecorated" look just emerging in the States.

Equally inviting was the Sutton Square drawing room Stacey designed for Harold and Alice Guinzburg, close friends of the Cheneys. For Harold Guinzburg, the publisher of Vita Sackville-West, Thorstein Veblen, and James Joyce, Stacey experimented with new color tonalities while assembling a living room verging, appropriately, on a library. Starting with his classic monochromatic perimeter—here, celadon walls, off-white curtains, and a beige rug—Stacey added clear turquoise and cerise then softened the palette with terra-cotta moldings (making the bookcases the focal point of the room) and a gray-green trumeau mirror. To lure readers and conver-

For Viking Press publisher Harold Guinzburg, Stacey experimented with new color tonalities while assembling a living room verging, appropriately, on a library. Starting with his classic monochromatic perimeter—here, celadon walls, off-white curtains, celadon rug—Stacey added clear turquoise and cerise, then softened the palette with terra-cotta moldings, making the bookcases the focal point of the room (and an inspiration for Mario Buatta). To lure readers and conversationalists alike, a pair of deep chaise longues flanks the fireplace.

sationalists alike, a pair of deep chaise longues flank the fireplace, while the jewellike verre églomisé miniatures and sconces framing the mirror, the sharp black accent of a Chinese lacquer box, unmatched chairs, a Louis XVI prie-dieu, green painted Italian neoclassic chairs, a Genovese painted writing table, and a T'ang period figure add a well-traveled mien. In the mirror one sees still more bookcases and a telltale Stacey signature, the sparkle of crystal suspended from a candelabra with tall tapered candles. (Incidentally, just prior to her marriage, Grace Kelly attended the wedding of her soon-to-be bridesmaid actress Rita Gam and Thomas Guinzburg in this room. And in the cozy way that the world once operated, soon the young Thomas Guinzburgs would also avail themselves of Stacey's services.)

Just as books naturally supplied the theme for Stacey's design for the Guinzburgs, statesmanship and understatement underscored the townhouse on East

81st Street that Marie and Averell Harriman settled into upon their return from several years in Paris with the Marshall Plan. Although Averell Harriman did succumb from time to time to a great Picasso or a fine piece of furniture, he was nearly as famous for his spartan taste and dislike of ostentation as he was for his considerable skill as a negotiator. Despite her sophistication, the congenial Marie equally loathed pretension, favoring a mix of modern pieces with French antiques, unfussy window treatments (fortunately Stacey's preference, too), and down-to-earth rooms that would withstand the demands of constant entertaining. For such clients, reminiscent of the Whitneys in their natural discretion, Stacey was the perfect match: although he had a point of view, he was not an authoritarian designer (or personality for that matter) and proved an easy collaborator. (It was a quality that endeared Stacey to Marie Harriman. In turn, her fondness fostered a confident Stacey whom pianist and bandleader Peter Duchin, an integral part of the Harriman household, remembers as wry, clever, and endlessly amusing—in short, excellent company.) Of course, with the Harrimans there was one very special—and not in the least bit understated—consideration: an art collection that included two Van Goghs, six Cézannes, two Picassos, three Matisses, six Derains, a Gauguin, a Seurat, and a Degas ballerina that would make any designer look good.

Coolly injecting style within the framework of his clients' requirements, Stacey's stylistic punch had an unusual effect on children. Echoing the imagery used by the Isles children to describe Stacey's work, Marie Harriman's granddaughter, Alida Morgan, described the dashing entrance hall of the Harriman house as a slightly intimidating, magical *Alice in Wonderland*–style environment where she and her sister played hopscotch on the overscaled black-and-white checkerboard floor and coasted down the banister under the gaze of Degas's beribboned *Petite Danseuse de Quatorze Ans*. Beyond was a smart French-style graveled garden complete with a wrought-iron table and the occasional pigeon.

With art-gallery celadon walls and seating furniture in deep red and rhododendron green (changed to slipcovers of pale rose and lichen in the spring), the living room was designed expressly to showcase paintings as well as politics. The room was the collaboration of a triumvirate: Marie Harriman's superb paintings (including the showstopping Picasso *Woman with a Fan* that

had graced her former "disappearing dining room") and Averell Harriman's splurge on the impressive Louis XV console, purchased under Stacey's advisement, all woven together by Stacey with bits of satin, lacquer, mirror, a few French pieces, and practical—i.e., canine—considerations into a polished, if somewhat reticent, room. There is no question, however, that Stacey had hit his mark: even Brum, the Harrimans' Labrador, appears comfortable amongst the finery of the Harriman living room—ample evidence that Stacey had pleased his straightforward clients.

Across the hall was a more intimate sitting room, occasionally used as the women's post-dinner withdrawing room when men discussed politics over cognac and cigars in the dining room. Perhaps in compensation for the forgone conversation, the room of French furniture, mirrors, and a delicate palette departed from the customary unfussy Harriman aesthetic: it has been described as "pure Stacey" in its drama and style. Similar contrasts played out upstairs. Averell's bedroom, with an ensuite dressing room of Jean-Michel Frank–inspired built-ins, was characteristically monastic, while Marie's bedroom was a glorious moderne confection of blue silk, French chairs, a mirrored dressing table, boudoir pillows, and Picassos. Stacey clearly excelled at turning out bedrooms that were feminine sanctuaries, and Marie, a habitual late riser who was very likely to start her day phoning from her bed, made good use of this talent both in New York City and Sands Point, New York.

Originally purchased as a way station to change clothes between polo matches at Meadow Brook, the rambling Harriman bungalow in Sands Point epitomized the lack of pretension so valued by the couple. By the 1950s, the Harrimans had added a pool, a croquet course, a tennis court, and a dock, transforming the low-slung house sandwiched between the Guggenheim and Swope properties into a full-fledged summer residence, where friends and grandchildren alike were welcome. Under Stacey's usual light touch, the house retained its easygoing deco interiors, but it inevitably acquired a few grace notes. Redolent of the boxwood that defined the garden, the eclectic porch with long mirrored table, rag rug, and deep St. Thomas sofa (remembered as the size of a queen bed!) piled with cushions doubled as a summer dining room. Banquettes, having proved their worth in the Harriman duplex on East 68th Street, now made their appearance with card tables in the corners of the more formal living room. Even the comfortable garden furniture chicly dressed in pale blue sailcloth—the chaises fitted with pale blue awnings to protect Marie's delicate eyes from the sun—didn't escape Stacey's ministrations. The airy blue and white Porthault bedroom where Marie would hold court dressed in a gorgeous bed jacket was, in the perceptive eyes of future design editor Wendy Goodman, "the most glamorous bedroom in the world!"

The Harrimans' Hobe Sound house, distinguished by a pecky cypress living room and travertine floors, was the warm-climate version of their Sands Point residence. The living room mixed comfortable sofas with glass-top tables, while a towering secretary packed with lettuce-green majolica served as a focal point for the room. Adjacent to the living room was a dark green and bamboo card room for the bridge-loving Harrimans. Outdoors, canopied chaises were dressed in pastel sailcloth—over the years, they were covered in a variety of colors, from pale blue to pink to pistachio. As always, everything was low-key and comfortable, but there was one surefire sign that Stacey had had a hand in the design: the dining room had a nightclub–style layout of banquettes along the walls with mirror-topped, pickled café tables with bell pendants on the corners (the resort version of Frances Cheney's gilded chinoiserie café tables) and a long center table for buffets.

When Averell Harriman took office as governor of New York in 1955, Marie acerbically described the interiors of the depressing governor's mansion as "Early Halloween," a fact that would have made no difference if the Harrimans, like their predecessors, had planned to live primarily in New York City. But the Harrimans actually moved to Albany to mix, entertain, and promote Averell's ambitious political agenda. As the rambling Queen Anne house assumed new importance with the change of administration, Harriman brought Stacey to Albany, where he warmed dreary rooms with lively pastels and prints, strategically dressed windows, configured seating to foster conversation, emphasized a few key antiques, and hung the Harrimans' famous paintings, all with a sharp eye on the budget. Alida Morgan and Peter Duchin both recall that Averell Harriman, pleased with the results, would henceforth call Stacey his "Minister of the Interior."

While work on the governor's house may have been prestigious, the inventive Stacey surpassed himself on projects for young clients, where his flair and antiquarian skills combined to great advantage. Typically, he would seek out one very unusual and beautiful element to define a room (there was rarely room in a youthful budget for many Stacey antiques) then build his design around this exquisite find to dazzling effect.

Though he did succumb from time to time to a great Picasso or fine antique, Averell Harriman (opposite) was as famous for his spartan taste as for his diplomatic skills. Marie Harriman loathed pretension and required interiors that stood up to dogs and heavy entertaining. For such clients, reminiscent of the Whitneys in their natural discretion, Stacey was perfectly matched: authoritarian neither as a designer nor as a personality, he easily accommodated client parameters. Of course, there was a very special consideration when working for the Harrimans: a superlative art collection of Van Goghs, Cézannes, two Picassos, three Matisses, Derains, a Gauguin, a Seurat, and a Degas ballerina that would make any designer shine. Harriman would shortly enlist Stacey's services to update the governor's mansion in Albany, referring to Stacey as his "Minister of the Interior."

Betty Sherrill, then a young assistant at McMillen (and now its illustrious chairwoman), remembers visiting a Yale classmate of her husband's who, with his new bride, had hired Stacey to design their apartment; the designer had flanked a sofa with eighteenth-century pedestals surmounted with shimmering rock-crystal girandoles. The dramatic statement required little more than a quiet background and beautifully made custom upholstery for a high-style living room.

As the decade unfolded, France increasingly claimed Stacey's time. He extended his roots into the Île-de-France, where he signed a lease on an abandoned Louis XIII château in 1956. Based on a design by the sixteenth-century architect Jacques I Androuet du Cerceau, the rambling Château de Neuville had suffered greatly during war, occupation, and lesser

B*ased on a design by the sixteenth-century architect Jacques I Androuet du Cerceau, Stacey's rambling Château de Neuville (opposite) had great bones and indestructible beauty, despite the ravages of war and the occupation. If Paris was a retreat for Stacey, the château in the Yvelines was a haven. Its endless views, timeless stone floors, vast calm, and immense beauty—as well as immense demands—supplied Stacey with a quiet venue, a purpose, and more. According to Albert Hadley, the château was Stacey's great love.*

transient hazards; great bones, however, lent it indestructible beauty. Its tranquil endurance, enfilade floor plan, and grave dignity would be irresistible to most, but particularly to someone of Stacey's temperament, training, and talent. If Paris was a retreat, the château outside the town of Gambais was a haven. Its endless views, timeless stone floors, vast calm, and immense beauty—as well as immense demands—supplied George with a quiet venue, a purpose, and more: according to Albert Hadley, the château was Stacey's great love.

Stacey undertook the reclamation of the Château de Neuville as an avocation, an opportunity to pursue his favorite pastimes of finding antiques and assembling beautiful rooms. Decorating one room at a time—in fact, he never seemed to progress beyond a few grand reception rooms that more than adequately took care of his needs—he brought the château back to life. When money was needed for a major renovation, such as the

repair of the extensive slate roof, the château was simply rented out as the location for the film *La Vie de Château* with Catherine Deneuve. (More recently, *Peau d'Âne*, *Les Liaisons Dangereuses*, and *Ridicule*, were filmed at the château.)

Most of the time, Stacey pursued his own quirky rhythms while at the château, puttering with the interiors and in the garden, hunting down antiques, making the rounds of the local tradespeople, taking coffee in the local café, and touring the countryside in his elegant French convertible of the moment, often a rare Delage or a Delahaye model. Anne Cheney Zinsser remembers visiting the neighboring town of Gambais with George and observing how thoroughly he had endeared himself to the townspeople and how he engaged in conversation with the butcher, the boulangère, and the milkman with an ease so much at odds with his social discomfort among peers. At this time, in near-beatnik fashion, Stacey began to wear his trademark all-black ensembles, and locals still laugh about the time the somberly dressed Stacey was mistaken for a priest and approached for a blessing. Despite having fostered bonds with the local tradespeople, the retiring Stacey was not given to conventional social entertainments, house parties, or sports at the local club and lived for the most part a shy, hermit-like existence at the château. Nevertheless, he was proud of his château and loved to share it with those who would appreciate it. He invited designers Billy Baldwin and Albert Hadley, as well as assorted Davisons and Cheneys, to visit. When Baldwin had to turn down an invitation to the château, Stacey, who had long ago perfected wit as a defense mechanism, replied, "I know you always stay with the *Windsors* when you come to France."

Vogue augmented the mystique Stacey was accruing as an "all-American aristocrat" when it published the Château de Neuville in 1956. The decoration of the château was classic Stacey once again: not slavishly academic, but respectful, refined, and independent. Making the most of the splendid architecture, stone floors, and graceful room placement, Stacey's decoration highlighted the compelling architecture. He left the old floors elegantly bare, placed furniture in an orderly, slightly spare fashion, and addressed scale with tall mirrors, paintings, wall *appliques*, pedestals, and even a rack of antlers to emphasize the inherent spaciousness. Besides his usual battery of neoclassical

attributes—Louis XVI furniture, bouillotte lamps, urns, sconces, and busts—Stacey added easy incongruities that brought charm to an imposing space, including a mix of flowered linen and damask, a curious low coffee table, curtains that did not match within the same room (surprisingly, the yellow silk and puce velvet curtains looked rather good together), and clear varied colors ("the expected reds as well as green damask," noted *Vogue*) alternating with the bright notes of yellow and turquoise opaline glass. Remarkably, after years of reconsidering dining rooms, Stacey settled for a long table surrounded by Louis XVI chairs in his own house.

The decoration of the château (overleaf) was classic Stacey: not slavishly academic, but respectful, refined, and independent. Given the splendid architecture, stone floors, and graceful enfilade layout, Stacey left the old floors elegantly bare, placed furniture in an orderly, slightly spare fashion, and addressed scale with tall mirrors, paintings, wall sconces, pedestals, and even a rack of antlers to emphasize the inherent spaciousness. In deference to the architecture, Stacey relinquished his experimentation with dining arrangements to produce a classic salle à manger at the Château de Neuville.

Stacey was proud of his château and loved to share it with those who would appreciate it, inviting designers Billy Baldwin and Albert Hadley and assorted Davisons and Cheneys to visit. When Baldwin had to turn down an invitation to the château, Stacey, who had long ago perfected wit as a defense mechanism, riposted, "I know you always stay with the Windsors when you come to France."

In the main salon at the Château de Neuville, Stacey blended decorative elements with important pieces (the bust ultimately was acquired by the Metropolitan Museum of Art in New York), buttressed by his respect for architecture and adherence to symmetric placement. Gilt-wood architectural elements show up repeatedly in Stacey's work from the 1950s. The pair of mandarin figures on the chest recalls Stacey's early collaboration with Frances Cheney.

As Stacey spent more time in France, he acquired new friends, including the fashion photographer Henry Clarke (opposite), who would later be celebrated as the creator of Vreeland's exotic travel-fashion shoots. Here, the young Clarke mischievously photographs himself, immobilized by beauty, in the London Vogue studio.

Clarke lived not far from Stacey on the rue Bonaparte (above). Nearby, too, on the rue Jacob was L'Aigle, the antique store of Clarke's partner, Raymond Poteau. A glance at Clarke's apartment shows the visual affinity of the three men. The red leather voyeuse is nearly identical to one that appears in Stacey's own Paris apartment (see page 150).

Spending more time in France, Stacey now began to develop new friends. Included in his circle was an eccentric art historian, Richard Carrott, who owned the neighboring La Tourelle in Rochefort, where dinner parties could last throughout the night; antique dealer Jean-Louis Raynaud and his family; and Raymond Poteau, who owned the well-regarded antique store L'Aigle on the rue Jacob in Paris. Based on photographs of Poteau's house, L'Aumônière in Roquebrune, filled with baluster urns, busts, drawings, lamps, Louis XVI desks, and tôle flowers that exude Stacey style, it seems likely that Stacey kept a close watch on the inventory at L'Aigle. At heart still an antiques dealer, Stacey had a habit of stopping in a store to chat, swap stories, and examine objects, which helped him create an easy rapport with *antiquaires*, and it was probably through such circumstances that he came to know Poteau.

Raymond Poteau's partner was the *Vogue* photographer Henry Clarke, who in Paris lived not far from Stacey in a charming attic apartment on the rue Bonaparte. Looking at Clarke's apartment, the visual affinity between Clarke, Poteau, and Stacey is obvious. With the palette of red and green enlivened by bright yellow against white walls, one might wonder whether Stacey advised on the colors while Poteau supplied the antiques. Interestingly, the selection of furniture and neoclassical objects—the bouillotte lamp, bust, girandole, armillary sphere, bookcase, and a hint-of-Louis-XVI armchair in the foreground—might just as easily have been chosen by Stacey, while the red leather *voyeuse* is strikingly similar to one that appears in the photograph of Stacey's own Paris apartment.

It seems the three took excursions out of Paris, where Henry Clarke's lens captured Stacey predictably accessorized with hat and cigarette, but in a rare relaxed mood. If the photo of a fey Stacey is unusual and appealing, the scribble on the back is equally so, suggesting that the photographer, like many others, had been subject to the teasing raillery of Stacey. Ostensibly the famous photographer of Suzy Parker, Dorian Leigh, and Veruschka and the future genius behind Vreeland's iconic fashion travelogues for *Vogue* wrote self-deprecatingly, "Perfectly vicious print. I am sorry—but I still have great troubles in the darkroom. No cracks from you, Bud!"

Stacey's designs and Helen Marshall's paintings continued to reveal their parallel themes. As Marshall's painting career flourished with three shows

at the influential Durlacher Brothers gallery on 57th Street, inclusion in the Whitney Annual, the Corcoran Biennial, and an exhibition at the Museum of Modern Art, *ARTnews* described her paintings in terms that might have easily applied to the Levy and Cheney drawing rooms, commenting on the elegant simplification, sophisticated color, and structural formality of her work. The critics also noted the underlying poise displayed by Marshall's work and her ability to determine and pursue an objective: "Her paintings express intelligence and control. She knows what she wants to do, and she finds out how to do it." The same could be said of Marshall's personal life, where she confidently cobbled together a happy but unconventional existence as an exhibiting artist, academic, and wife traversing two continents.

In contrast to Helen Marshall, Stacey could not integrate his life into a cohesive whole. When a young member of the Davison clan came to study in Paris, Stacey gingerly assumed the role of guardian. Having helped James Davison find an apartment in his own building at 1, rue de la Chaise, Stacey assiduously kept an eye on his young charge, formally having him in for cocktails and updates but never, never including him in his Paris activities nor introducing him among his friends. (Davison's real introduction to lively, local Paris came not from the stiff Stacey but from his family's high-spirited former chauffeur, a White Russian then living in the Fifteenth Arrondissement.)

On an outing to the château with his aunt and uncle, Frances and Ward Cheney, Davison intuited the explanation for Stacey's secretive behavior: there was a young man in Stacey's life, a fact that Stacey was evidently uncomfortable revealing. This attractive young man, whom Davison had also sighted in Paris, hovered in the background where he was occasionally glimpsed in passing but was never introduced to the guests and never joined the luncheon party. The shadowy Billy (no last name known) made appearances in photos over several years—picnicking near the château (a box of Lucky Strikes prominent among the picnic fare of bread, wine, and *saucisse*), walking near Notre Dame, relaxing at the beach, touring in Morocco—clearly more than a passing apparition in Stacey's life. The photos remained in Stacey's possession until the end of his life, but Billy was never brought to the attention of even as close a friend as Frances Cheney. The poise, as ever, was all in the design.

The camera's eye captured a relaxed Stacey (opposite) predictably accessorized with hat and cigarette. If the photo of a fey Stacey is unusual and appealing, so too is the self-deprecating scribble on the back that suggests that Henry Clarke, like many others, knew firsthand the teasing raillery of Stacey. The famous photographer of Suzy Parker, Dorian Leigh, and Veruschka wrote disarmingly, "Perfectly vicious print. I am sorry—but I still have great troubles in the darkroom. No cracks from you, Bud!"

The shadowy Billy (below)—last name unknown—makes appearances in photos over several years.

CHAPTER TEN

THE GRAND MASTER

1960–1975

After decades of discovery, experimentation, and response to nuances of mood, Stacey's style crystallized into its final balanced form in the 1960s. The easy mix of clear color, French furniture, sleek coffee tables, lacquer, Venetian mirrors, and modern upholstery that Stacey had pioneered was now a given for sophisticated rooms across America. In the versatility of his later work, which ranges from a contemporary sitting room for Princess Grace to an understated drawing room for Ava Gardner to the disarmingly sumptuous cottage that would be his final French country house, Stacey exhibits complete late-career composure. At a time when Parsons School of Design jettisoned the historically oriented curriculum championed by Parsons and Odom to refashion itself as a school of environmental design, and younger decorators flirted with Lucite, paisley, conversation pits, and hanging basket chairs, Stacey serenely followed his own proven course, increasingly focused on eighteenth-century French furniture, his time-honored source of inspiration.

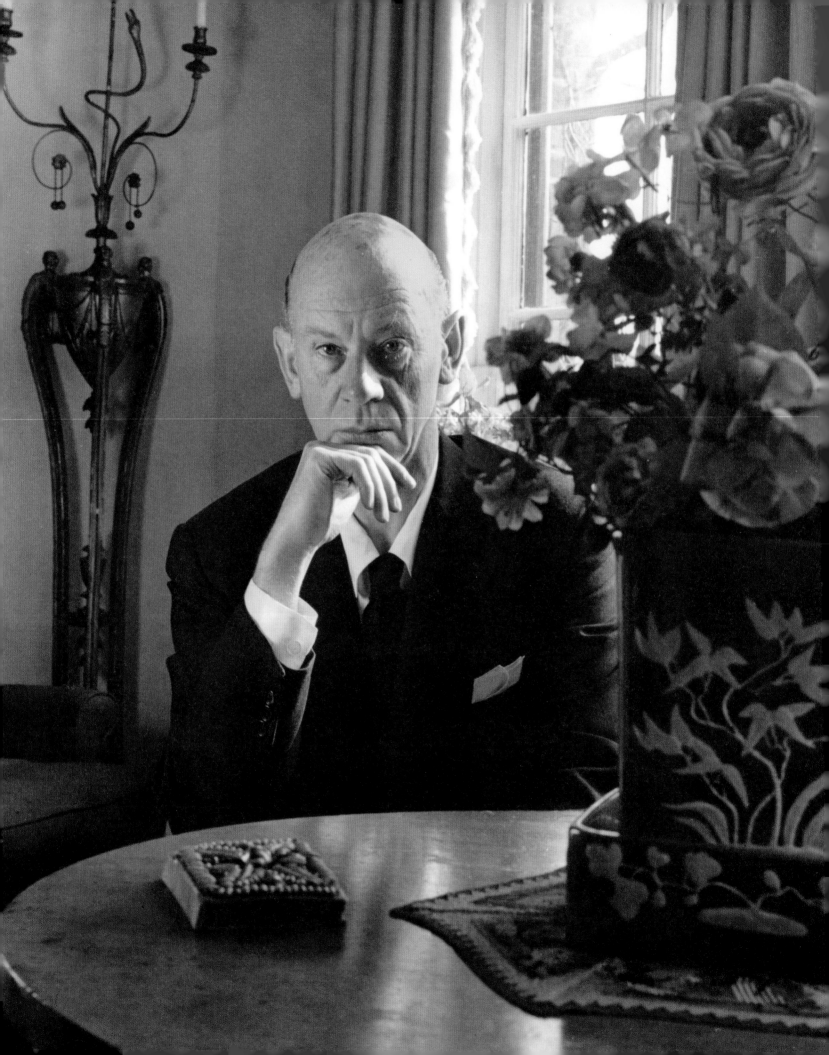

Well-heeled clients in New York, the Hamptons, Westchester, Arizona, Monaco, London, and Paris came to Stacey, and often one glamorous client led to another. That was the case with Princess Grace and Ava Gardner, who had been friends since the filming of *Mogambo*. In the 1950s, Gardner had removed herself from Hollywood, and perhaps taxes as well, by settling in a villa outside of Madrid. But a lively spirit like Gardner's could hardly flourish in a quiet location, and she had just obtained an apartment in the center of town, coincidentally next door to the exiled Juan Perón. With Stacey spending more and more time in Europe, it was natural for the princess to suggest that Stacey help Gardner decorate her elegant new apartment in Madrid. The distasteful neighbor notwithstanding, Stacey designed an apartment with grandeur and restraint worthy of the Hapsburgs, so pleasing Gardner that he was eventually hired to decorate her house and apartment in London. Starting with a symmetrical floor plan underscored by pairs of urns, pedestals, lamps, and fauteuils, Stacey built a color scheme of dove gray walls and curtains anchored with espresso damask on the primary seating and dramatized with gilt-wood chairs covered in crimson and in yellow. In addition to the gilt-wood Louis XVI chairs, he assembled gilded architectural fragments above the mantel and bookcases and gilt-bronze candelabra for a discreet sparkling effect. The artfully arranged walls, filled with well-proportioned paintings generally hung in pairs and flanked by sconces, urns, wood fragments, and books, showcase Stacey's gift for composition.

As Stacey did with so many of his accomplished, stylish clients, he developed an easy friendship with Gardner. They bonded over the fact that both had feckless, gentle fathers, and while Stacey and Gardner had moved on to more sophisticated lives, they had both retained an essential simplicity honed in their childhoods. The actress loved to visit Stacey at his later country house, Le Poulailler, and nostalgically run barefoot in the fields as she had once run across the tobacco fields worked by her father, a tenant farmer. For his part, Stacey was often the recipient of Gardner's hospitality in Madrid, where he would escort her to dinner parties and witness her colorful life from a ringside seat. In later years, he especially enjoyed recounting a story of Gardner flouncing out of a dinner party where she felt slighted by the hostess and commandeering the most handsome footman on her way out the door; Stacey the raconteur always ended the story with the same flourish: "And right now, there is an old man somewhere in Spain boasting at the *taberna* of his night with Ava Gardner."

The Ava Gardner association provides a window into Stacey the professional. Unlike the impractical Alford Stacey, George Stacey ran a tight business with an astute Yankee eye trained on profitability. As a one-man office, Stacey worked in an efficient, no-nonsense manner. He designed, specified, and oversaw his projects; clients would pay directly for labor, material, and antiques; a design fee was assessed. Jess Morgan, Ava Gardner's longtime financial manager, remembers a cordial professional relationship, neat, whistle-clean bookkeeping, and a definite sense of Stacey "expecting and wanting to be paid." And although Stacey loved a good story, he was also admirably discreet. One of the Davison clan recalls a

B y the 1960s, the eclectic mix of French furniture, sleek coffee tables, lacquer, Venetian mirrors, and modern upholstery that Stacey had pioneered was a given for sophisticated rooms across America. While younger decorators began to experiment with Lucite, paisley, and hanging basket chairs, Stacey serenely followed his own proven course and increasingly focused on eighteenth-century French furniture, his time-honored source of inspiration.

croquet game interrupted when Stacey received a phone call from the ailing Gardner, who by that time had developed a reputation as a notorious alcoholic. Whoever had called Stacey to the phone had identified the caller, but when Stacey returned to the game and his expectant companions, he would only comment in a general fashion on the phone call, alluding neither to Gardner's condition nor to the designs underway.

Stacey always had time for the loyal Princess Grace, who kept him updated on her busy life via postcards, quick notes, and photos. Changes in family life prompted additional design work, pleasantly justifying more time spent in Europe. When the princess acquired a country house at Roc Agel, in France, Stacey helped with the interiors and applied his skill with wall arrangements to hanging Hollywood memorabilia in the private quarters. As Stacey had with Ward Cheney and Averell Harriman, he developed his own camaraderie with Prince Rainier, and they exchanged teasing

S tacey's living room for Ava Gardner in Madrid (above) achieved grandeur and restraint worthy of the Hapsburgs. The room pivots on the powerful rhythm of pairs and a sober scheme of dove gray walls and espresso damask enlivened with shots of vermillion and sunflower. Bronze dorée candelabra and gilt-wood Louis XVI chairs and architectural fragments discreetly sparkle.

Gilt bouquets flirt with somber Spanish paintings in Ava Gardner's persimmon-glazed dining room (opposite). Tension of a more political nature unfurled on the balcony, where Gardner, armed with her naughtiest Spanish, constituted an opposition party of one against the arm-waving comeback speeches that her next-door neighbor, exiled dictator Juan Perón, rehearsed from his own balcony.

At the Palais Princier in Monaco, Stacey created a conservatory-cum–family room, addressing the lofty scale of the windowed space with a towering Coromandel screen, a generous borne, and a hefty writing table. In addition to supplying a telescope that could be used to eye the glamorous comings and goings in the harbor, Stacey found an unobtrusive spot for the princess' Oscar for The Country Girl.

notes and light updates from time to time. Writing to thank Stacey for design work on his boat, Rainier added a jaunty conspiratorial aside as one heavy smoker and car buff to another: "I am off to Paris by road driving this silly little car of mine: the Rolls-Royce! (The ashtray is already full!)"

By the 1970s, the active young family needed a family sitting room, as well as studies for the children rather than a nursery. A palace renovation that placed Stacey in charge of decoration was launched. The striking result was an airy garden room that doubled as the family room, classic Stacey in its easy assimilation of antiques within a modernist space. Always attentive to scale, Stacey acquired oversized pieces for the soaring room, including a lofty Coromandel screen, a generous borne, now completely shed of its Victorian pedigree, and a rustic writing table to structure the space. For color, he ventured into a rare palette of off-whites. Among the plants, garden bench, glass-and-brass tables, chessboard, and telescope for keeping an eye on the glamorous goings-on in the harbor, Stacey found an unobtrusive spot for Princess Grace's Oscar for The Country Girl. Later, as the family began to spend more time in Paris for the purpose of the children's schooling, Stacey also designed the family's new, larger apartment on the Avenue Foch.

The most self-assured and daring of all of Stacey's late-career assemblages was without question his new country house in France. When the twelve-year lease on the Château de Neuville came due, members of the Labriffe family, who had owned the château since the eighteenth century, were ready to reclaim their house, which was now much spruced up and much less forlorn. Once again, the Raynauds offered a housing solution, albeit a somewhat unpromising one: a former chicken coop on their own country property where Jean-Louis had once stored and restored his antique inventory. Having mastered quirky stylishness in the Peacock Point squash court, Stacey had no problem decorating Le Poulailler and simply made of it yet another handy foil for his particular brand of chic.

Using the trussed ceiling, rough plastered walls, and brick floor to full counter advantage, Stacey casually placed his château furniture—the familiar bookcase, the yellow Louis XVI chair, the Régence chair (now re-covered in green moiré), the tôle flowers in urns, the bouillotte lamps—in these improbable surroundings. He intuitively understood the seductive interplay

of rough-hewn and gilded surfaces, primitive and polished elements, and in the process created the template for future exercises in rustic and refined contrasts by Michael Taylor in California, and years later, Stephen Sills in Bedford, New York. Another young member of the extended Peacock Point family recalls a visit to Houdan, where Stacey welcomed his visitors to his humble converted chicken coop, indicating an unprepossessing door, and suggested they "just have a look around." As Stacey had intended, his visitors were speechless with awe when they beheld the elegant room, which he had polished to perfection in anticipation of their visit. Other visitors came, too, including Anne Cheney Zinsser, of course, as well as Ava Gardner, Princess Grace and her daughters, Mario Buatta, Ethel Smith and Betty Sherrill of McMillen, and editors of *House & Garden*.

Though Stacey visited the States less frequently, he found time to design a Sutton Square townhouse, a villa in Arizona, and a casual beach house in East Hampton for Frances Cheney; a country house of chinoiserie, Porthault linens, and Louis XVI furniture for Joan Lord, Marie Harriman's sister; a Park Avenue apartment with his hallmark Coromandel screens, bronze dorée candelabra, and cherry red upholstery for Sylvia and Ralph Ablon. Peacock Point and its freewheeling extended family remained central to Stacey's life. In addition to the various Davisons, Cheneys, and Gateses, there was always an exotic assortment of family and quasi-family for amusement, ranging from exotic French cousins-by-marriage including Luc Bouchage and his boyfriend, Jean Schlumberger, the Tiffany jewelry designer, White Russian émigrés, croquet players of all generations and—by this point—Frances' grandchildren, who for the most part share Frederick P. Victoria's son's memories of Stacey as a highly forbidding presence.

H*aving mastered quirky stylishness in the Peacock Point squash court, Stacey had no problem decorating a former chicken coop. Playing off exposed ceiling trusses, rough plaster walls, and brick floor, Stacey's château furniture shone in its new surroundings. The seductive interplay of rough-hewn and gilded surfaces, primitive and refined elements created a template for future exercises in rustic contrast by Michael Taylor in California and, many years later, Stephen Sills in Bedford, New York.*

O nce transitioned from chicken coop to human abode, Le Poulailler happily adapted to its new identity (left and below). After Stacey departed, Parisian architect Alain Raynaud, the son of Stacey's old friend, the antique dealer Jean-Louis Raynaud, continued the heritage of chic with his own stylish renovation. The garden bench (above) was the frequent rendezous point for Stacey and the caretaker's children.

Even in the warm environment provided by the Davison-Cheney clan, Stacey could be difficult. When Gates Davison, Frances Cheney's cousin, brought the young Mario Buatta for drinks in the 1960s, Stacey slighted the younger designer's admiring overtures. Ironically, Stacey *was* interested in the career of the rising Mario Buatta and silently followed his work. He even methodically updated his address book entry for Buatta with each move, but his own awkwardness prevented him from establishing a friendship.

Given such torturous reticence, it is not surprising that when Frances Cheney died in 1968, Stacey did not express outward grief for his muse, champion, and friend, even to her family. Either as a Yankee from rock-hardened Connecticut, he had simply never allowed his feelings to gain currency, or many, many years ago, Stacey had removed himself from the painful world of articulated emotion, neatly substituting châteaux and sconces for shared expressions of the soul.

O*verlooking the garden at Sutton Square, Frances Cheney's pale blue bedroom filled with French furniture was an oasis of calm. The continuous use of the blue and white print soothes the eye, while black lacquer and objets boost the elegance quotient. The chandelier appears to be one that previously hung in Cheney's Fifth Avenue master bedroom (page 93).*

CHAPTER ELEVEN

DENOUEMENT AND LEGACY

1975–1993

L ike a dignified opera star, Stacey orchestrated his retirement with his artistry intact. When he counseled young architect Alain Raynaud, the son of his old friend Jean-Louis Raynaud, to work only while still infused with passion, Stacey may well have been speaking to himself. For more than four decades, he had reflected changes in American temperament and taste in his designs, framing these shifts in moods within his own sensibility. This sensibility was based on classical ideas of proportion, symmetry, reason, scale, and historicism—the seminal Parsons School of Design training— which perfectly balanced his own inclination for experimentation and glamour. It was the poise between these two countervailing forces that created the distinctive sparkle of his style. In the aftermath of the Vietnam War, American taste, as politics, ran in an anti-Establishment direction, valuing novelty, ingenuousness, and personal dictates over the classical canons of design. While he would always be interested in new aesthetic influences, Stacey was incapable of following trends for the sake of mere fashion;

GEORGE STACEY AND THE CREATION OF AMERICAN CHIC

he worked from a central vision that lent his work coherence and elegance. Like Cristóbal Balenciaga, who, convinced couture as he loved it was dead, shuttered his couture house in 1968 during the Parisian student uprisings, Stacey did not find much repertoire to attract him.

It seemed the perfect moment to enjoy the immeasurable pleasures of life. Stacey was still sufficiently spry to spend extended months in France, where he fussed with his garden, strolled in Paris, chatted with shop owners, and stayed abreast of the news. His new apartment in Paris was at 88, rue de l'Université, still in the aristocratic Faubourg Saint-Germain, but it was Le Poulailler that drew him most strongly. Gardens and cats now fascinated him. His own garden was a perpetual source of pleasure; he proudly photographed flower beds at high season and traded notes with weekend gardeners on both sides of the Atlantic. The mysterious landscape of the Désert de Retz, an eighteenth-century private pleasure garden that had welcomed courtiers from Versailles and served as the precursor to Marie-Antoinette's Hameau de la Reine, exerted a melancholy pull on Stacey. Its calm recalled the timelessness of the Château de Neuville that had so appealed to him.

Designed as an eighteenth-century pleasure garden and escape for courtiers, the Désert de Retz outside of Paris inspired Marie Antoinette's gardens at Versailles. Beautiful, moody, elegiac, and erudite, the garden captivated Stacey at the end of his life. It had known sumptuous parties and far-reaching influence but now lay in disrepair.

When in New York, Stacey left his apartment at the Dorchester daily for a twenty-block walk, his gait now displaying a slight shuffle. During his rounds, he kept an eye on his favorite antique stores, smiling at the younger designers darting about their business. While his black and gold apartment did not need another bibelot, he polished and tended his antiques, which included a black lacquer commode signed by Pierre Migeon and a Georges Jacob *voyeuse*, with his customary love. He smoked incessantly—visitors say the air in his apartment was blue—and used, of course, a black cigarette holder. Mentally sharp, he continued to work the *New York Times* crossword puzzle daily, read biographies of Picasso and the travel writings of Paul

Theroux, and listen to Metropolitan Opera broadcasts. He was always planning his next visit to France.

Surprisingly, Stacey's shyness seemed to dissipate at this stage of his life. He became courtly, speaking considerately with the elderly women in his co-op and flirting with the desk staff, who fussed over him incessantly and made sure he took a scarf or umbrella as weather dictated. Alice Gates also lived at the Dorchester and provided ongoing camaraderie until her death in 1983. He kept up loose contact with long-term clients Averell Harriman and Prince Rainier. Commiserating with Stacey on the advance of time, Rainier wrote in his usual conspiratorial tone, "Monaco is doing very well, and 1989 was the forty-year mark for me being at the helm! Makes me feel VERY old!!"

B illy Baldwin captured Babe Paley's famous casual chic in his design for her pied-à-terre at the St. Regis Hotel. Like Stacey, Baldwin contrasted a simple cotton print for tenting with grand velvets, damask, and polished European furniture. The draped mirror that Stacey unveiled at 400 Park Avenue for Diana Vreeland became a leitmotif in Baldwin's repertoire, appearing in apartments for the Paleys, the Vreelands, and novelist Speed Lamkin.

So, the curt Yankee had become solicitous, and time and contentment seem to have softened some of Stacey's rough edges. Recalling his childhood, he assessed it philosophically, lightly brushing off the hardships and distress. ("Why, it didn't really hurt us," he would say.) He had a particular rapport with cats and nurtured any that wandered toward the squash court or his cottage in Houdan. With the exception of Frances Cheney's granddaughter Lisa von Ziegesar, with whom he had a tender relationship (she was possibly the only person ever seen holding hands with Stacey), Stacey had always been intimidating to children. Now he doted on the children of the caretaker of the Raynaud property in Houdan, bringing them bits of candy from the village, collecting their school photos and drawings, and playing with them in the garden. One of them grew up to become an architect, perhaps reflecting that early interest on the part of Stacey.

As the old order—Alice Gates, Brenda Frazier, Diana Vreeland, Frederick P. Victoria, Betsey Whitney,

Princess Grace, and Ava Gardner—exited, a younger admiring group befriended him. He loved the attention. Although Stacey always retained his laconic style of speech, he excelled at the art of conversation, especially the variety incorporating raillery and bons mots, when surrounded by friends. In favorable circumstances, he held court, recounting choice bits from a fund of witty anecdotes; he often announced in advance, "Now this is a *really* good story," and expected full attention from his rapt audience. John Humpstone, the owner of the attractive boutique Lexington Gardens, as well as a member of the extended Davison clan, would stop by with Doug Wright for cocktails accompanied by stories of time spent in Venice, Madrid, Monaco, and Paris. While the drinks were stiff, the food was indifferent: Doug Wright remembers that at best, a few potato chips might appear. Of course, design was always the centerpiece of conversation, and Stacey often showed them rare books on design and reviewed fabric samples with them. Frances Cheney's daughter Anne Zinsser shared poetry with him and had him to weekly dinners. Mark Hampton and his wife, Duane, frequently invited him to dinner also. He kept a surreptitious watch on the work of Mario Buatta in New York and Alain Demachy in Paris, as these two designers' gift for color and fantasy had caught his appraising eye. He also admired the color transpositions and tablescapes of David Hicks.

He drove out to Peacock Point on weekends (except when ice daunted him in the winter), first in a Jaguar and later in a Mercedes-Benz convertible coupe. There, he would wander about the compound, now bereft of Mrs. Davison and the Cheneys but busy with a new generation. Just as he would drop in unannounced on Ruby Ross Wood and McMillen years earlier, he was known at Peacock Point for materializing out of nowhere for a chat. When young Harry Davison and his European wife built and decorated a new house on the property, he silently but keenly followed the progress. He was cranky when he witnessed the inevitable changes that would come to his beloved Octagon House after the Cheney era. Occasionally, he could still find a game of croquet. Athletic members of the family wondered impatiently when he would vacate their squash court.

Gradually, the trips to Locust Valley and France became fewer and fewer. Driving became a little precarious; Gates Davison no longer dared accept his

offers of lifts to the country. Stacey's lanky physique became brittle and thin. But the walks, the repartee, and joining friends for dinner continued. (As did the lingering legend: as late as the 1990s, Mrs. Frank H. Wyman dreamily reminisced that as a young married matron, she had had a twenty-two-room apartment on Fifth Avenue decorated by George Stacey and a sable coat—heaven!)

One day, Stacey suffered a fainting spell and collapsed onto the sidewalk. After that, he quickly deteriorated, and he died on June 24, 1993, at the age of

In the 1960s Michael Taylor (also a devotee of antique dealer Frederick P. Victoria) reinterpreted the black-and-white floor and clear colors of Château de Neuville into a smart Technicolor card room in San Francisco (opposite).

Mark Hampton's stylish library (above) riffs on the theme of chic—jazzed with white, neoclassicism, and red—played by Stacey in the Bermuda living room of Mr. and Mrs. Frank Wierdsma (see page 124).

Nick Olsen keeps a photo of Stacey's Paris apartment (page 150) in his inspiration file—and spins off casual feats of color, surprise, French furniture, and wall composition (above).

Stephen Sills (opposite) affirms Stacey's proposition that rusticity and elegance make exceptional bedfellows.

ninety-one. (Despite his accomplishments and sophisticated friends, he had retained a common touch to the end, and left his Mercedes coupe to his auto mechanic.) A memorial service at All Souls Church on the Upper East Side was attended by Stacey's few surviving friends and members of the Davison family. Stacey was buried where he would have felt most at home, surrounded by the lush rhododendrons of the Davisons' family plot in Locust Valley, near Frances and Ward Cheney, his clients, friends, and, ultimately, family. Fittingly, Helen Marshall and Hans van Nes, two of the friends with whom Stacey's great journey had begun, died the same year.

After eighty years of influence, assimilation, and imitation, the work of society decorator George Stacey looks classic and familiar to our eyes and no longer quite as revolutionary as it did when he first shot to prominence designing for iconoclastic It Girl Frances Cheney or fearless trendsetter Diana Vreeland in the 1930s. His unique style, an alliance of rigid classical training, New England restraint, Old World glamour, and the influence of a decade spent close to the aesthetic ferment of 1920s Paris, is pivotal to the story of modern design in America. His innovative rooms, with their offhand mix of period and provenance, interplay of grand and unassuming elements, and celebration of color and sensual fabric, challenged all prevailing conventions of good taste and set a new standard.

In turn, distinguished American designers, such as Sister Parish, Billy Baldwin, Mario Buatta, Michael Taylor, and Mark Hampton, adopted and modified elements of the Stacey style to create their own refined versions of American style. Others, too young to have heard of the Stacey mystique, have unconsciously absorbed the lessons and intuitively continue the arc of his work, increasing the iterations on now familiar themes: the play of contrast and highlighting of profiles, neutrals punched with jewel tones, touches of gilding, mirror, and crystal to render space seductive, the enduring standard of neoclassicism, and eighteenth-century furniture. The excitement Stacey brought to design was the recognition that design was not a didactic formula but a prism reflecting individuals and the moment. That long moment happened to be a golden age and, thanks to Stacey, it looked enormously chic.

F ollowing a tradition honed by Stacey, down-to-earth worldliness and
eclectic furnishings are now ingrained in American design. Maureen Footer
weaves silvery surfaces, a Mongolian lamb rug, glamorous mirrored tenting and
French, Swedish, and Italian antiques into a boudoir worthy of a modern Frances
Cheney (opposite). An inviting living room by Celerie Kemble (above) ups the
ante with the dazzle of a verre églomisé ceiling by artist Miriam Ellner.

With a nod to classicism, whiff of invention, and broad swathe of antiques, Carrier and Company Interiors adapts Stacey's fusion of modern edge with classical principles for contemporary living (left). The easy pairing of tavern table with silk curtains, white paint with old paneling, and patinated wood with industrial metal delivers understated—and timeless—elegance.

Tom Scheerer's brilliant design for the Lyford Cay Club affirms Stacey's tenets of symmetry, fantasy, and sparkle (opposite). Strong symmetrical furniture placement, a central chandelier, and confident daring in Scheerer's room update Stacey's insouciant 1934 design of the Cheney's Octagon House to the current century.

Stacey Style and the Stacey Estate

In Stacey's own possessions, the leitmotifs of his taste coalesce: lacquer, gilding, mirrors, or neoclassicism characterize nearly every decorative item he possessed. Most of his seating pieces, whether signed by Jacob, other master *menuisiers*, or not at all, have the simple lines of the Louis XVI or Directoire period. Seating provides the structure of a Stacey furniture plan, while items at eye level—gilt-wood chandeliers, mirrors, clocks, sconces, framed drawings, and paintings—typically provide the dazzle. As a master of contrast, Stacey offset the clean, simple lines of his chairs with refined ormolu and lacquer. His own apartment included gilded firedogs, inlaid Japanese tables, and an elegant lacquered Louis XV commode signed by Pierre Migeon. Incidental pieces were often custom-fabricated at Frederick P. Victoria. As it was the rare Stacey room that was complete without an elegant Coromandel screen lending dignity, chic, and height, Stacey possessed an imposing twelve-panel screen. Of course, he had a token blacka-moor in the form of an English porcelain figure. Classic Stacey rooms adhered to a time-honored color formula: monochrome walls, simple floor and window coverings (often in subdued tones) enlivened by jewel tone (famously red and green, with a strong yellow as a tertiary note) accents for upholstery, sparkling gilt wood, black lacquer for chic, and the dazzle of reflective mirrors, gilding, and crystal.

After Stacey's death in 1993, most furnishings from his New York apartment and country house were sold at Christie's, while Frederick P. Victoria and Son handled the sale of some of the most important items: the Coromandel screen, scagliola panels, and a Louis XVI secretary signed by Charles Topino. Stacey's French estate was settled by his longtime friend Marcelle Raynaud, widow of the Parisian antique dealer Jean-Louis Raynaud. Many of the smaller accessories and objets d'art—candelabra, gilt-wood fragments, framed drawings, low Japanese tables, the many pairs of urns so beloved by Stacey, and upholstered "Stacey chairs"—were distributed among friends.

1. A Louis XV commode, signed Migeon; Christie's lot 205, sale #7870, Important French Furniture, April 26, 1994. Though Stacey rarely veered toward the graceful curves of Louis XV, this piece justified an exception. The work of Pierre Migeon, a cabinetmaker beloved by Madame de Pompadour, is renowned for fine craftsmanship and beautiful proportions. The addition of Chinese lacquer panels satisfied Stacey's fondness for black. To his mind, as well as to Diana Vreeland's, black always injected a note of high-style sophistication.

2. An Empire ormolu chenet; Christie's lot 283, sale #7852, French and Continental Furniture, Objects of Art, and Carpets, March 24, 1994. Repeated use of gilt lent an overall shimmer to Stacey rooms, much the way the camera obscura provided Vermeer with a source for glinting light effects on his canvases. The clean, well-etched lines of Napoleonic design were a favorite of Stacey, who habitually developed his rooms from a strictly disciplined neoclassical base before introducing fabulous and fantastical elements for dash.

3. An Italian Baroque-style sixteen-light chandelier; Christie's lot 284, sale #7852, French and Continental Furniture, Objects of Art, and Carpets, March 24, 1994. Slightly rustic craftsmanship contrasted effectively with the refined objects and luxurious fabrics that were at home in a Stacey room. The gilt wood would certainly have appealed to Stacey, as would the fantastical carved tassel pendant.

4. A Louis XVI *voyeuse*, green-painted, stamped G Jacob; Christie's lot 287, sale #7852, French and Continental Furniture, Objects of Art, and Carpets, March 24, 1994. The stylish Directoire X-motif back, light painted finish, and humorously stubby legs of this late Jacob gaming stool are highly evocative of Stacey. The designer often chose painted, lacquered, and gilded finishes to introduce elements of light, chic, or sparkle to a room. Unembellished wood surfaces are rare in the Stacey repertory.

5. One of a pair of Italian baroque parcel-gilt side tables; Christie's lot 288, sale #7852, French and Continental Furniture, Objects of Art, and Carpets, March 24, 1994. French furniture supplemented by Italian and Asian pieces created depth and variety in Stacey's classical but non-doctrinaire designs. Both the bold outlines and robust carving satisfied Stacey's requirement for strong profiles. Italian furniture had been William Odom's special expertise, and Stacey probably acquired familiarity with the category through his association with Odom.

6. One of a pair of Louis XVI green-painted bergères, stamped Nadal L'Aine; Christie's lot 291, sale #7852, French and Continental Furniture, Objects of Art, and Carpets, March 24, 1994. Neoclassicism was the underpinning of a Stacey room, while pairs were favored for symmetry and used to create visual order in visually rich spaces. Stacey liked antiques that could be actively used in modern life. Chairmaker and joiner Nadal L'Aine provided deeply comfortable neoclassical chairs for an august clientele, including King Louis XVI (a large man) and his brother, the Comte d'Artois.

7. A Louis XV/XVI gilt-wood mirror, c. 1765; Christie's lot 275, sale #9090, French and Continental Furniture, Works of Art, Tapestries, and Carpets, March 30, 1999. Few Stacey rooms eluded the magic of a mirror. This model, like most of the mirrors Stacey chose, had a carved gilt-wood frame, which meant that it contributed sparkle from two sources: the gilt wood and the reflection of the mirror itself.

8. *Portrait of a Lady and a Gentleman on the Steps of a Château* by Anthelme-Francois Lagrenée; Christie's lot 3, sale #7828, Important and Fine Old Master Paintings, January 12, 1994. This slightly naïve, large painting with Empire subject matter probably appealed to the austere inclinations of Stacey. At the Château de Neuville, he hung baroque fantasies by Giuseppe Arcimboldo.

9. A pair of Blue John columns; Christie's lot 11, sale #9142, Important English Furniture, Objects of Art, and Carpets, April 22, 1999. Classical training and neoclassical objects, particularly in pairs, anchored the Stacey aesthetic. Pairs of urns, busts, columns, and obelisks inevitably found their way into Stacey's hands to exert cool order in luxurious spaces.

Writings by George Stacey

While Stacey's badinage in Vogue ("Paper the walls… and the grand piano. You may not like it, but then it will be too late") echoes in tone the concurrent advice of his client Diana Vreeland in her "Why Don't You…" column for Harper's Bazaar ("Have a dressing table hung with…carnations from Woolworth's tacked on casually"), it also provides practical decorating advice for American homemakers–definitely not Stacey's clients–caught between the Depression and the war.

Nestled among the witticisms and banter is advice from Stacey that emphasizes consideration of proportion, light, and balance and reveals his ongoing experiments with the conventional dining room. His suggestion for a terrace filled with Edwardian furniture recalls Carlos de Beistegui, who, as Stacey knew from a Harper's Bazaar issue of February 1938, filled his Parisian terrace with mantelpieces, gold mirrors, baroque commodes, painting, and carpets.

Make the Most of Your House

(*Vogue*, April 15, 1941)

Your house doesn't please you? You don't want to spend much money? You feel that something could be done? Treat your house or room as though you were a doctor. Study its weak points. Where it is dull, use bright colour; where it has too much light, tone down the colours. Make it a healthy place to live in, not a perfect picture; the perfect picture type usually dies on its feet.

Relax in one room after another and think about all the things that are fundamentally annoying; the proportions, the light, or perhaps the height. Balance is very important. If you need another window in the room to carry the colour or to build up a wall, fake it. Hang your curtains, and always keep them drawn. It may not be quite satisfactory in the daytime, but at night it is a sure-fire trick. If you have three windows in a row in a smallish room and you do want chintz or a figured material, curtain the two end windows in the figured stuff, and have the centre one in a plain material with coloured fringes that pick up colours in the end curtains. Or if you have two widely-spaced windows on the same wall and no important enough piece of furniture to place between them, fake a centre window. It is very effective.

Your room is perhaps too high? I can't believe it, but if you think it is, have your local handy man put in an inexpensive stock chair-rail, and paint the walls below a clear, dark colour, above a lighter colour. Paint the ceiling to match, avoiding whites above the eye-level. You'll practically stoop when you enter…. If the reverse is true, and you want to make the room higher, obviously a striped wall-paper is the simplest solution. The world is full of them, and very pretty they are. Perhaps your room is too long and narrow? If so, paper the two long walls in a large, flowered paper. Paint the two narrow ends a fine quiet colour to match a predominant shade in the paper. Break your room in the centre with two small sofas facing each other, with a low table, or perhaps a grand-scale desk or table, plunked in the centre of the room, to rivet your attention right there. On your floor, use three squares of carpet, and have the centre one a darker colour.

You have a large radio or grand piano that you have tried for years to make inconspicuous. You've gone through draping the piano, or trying to bend a little French screen around it, and the result still looked like a super-grand. The radio was just a fine upstanding piece of cabinetwork, and you couldn't put anything on it, anyway. Taking it for granted that you don't have both music-boxes in one room, of course, paper the walls, and piano or radio in a bright figured paper. (Your paper-hanger will fight you to the draw about pasting paper on that shining wood finish, but stick to it.) You may not like it, but then it will be too late, so you'd better like it. Anyway it can be scraped later, at great expense.

If you must plan your space carefully, you might forego a typical dining-room. Use one or two small tables with built-in seats, covered in bright colours. Put your piano in the dining-room, if you can get away with it. Be sure, however, that the light is not strong, for every one relaxes at table under a dim light. Use as much material in the hangings as you can afford. It kills noise, which helps the scintillating conversation of your friends.

Drape swags of material over the doors high up on the wall, and have another swag over the fireplace…making them, perhaps, of striped bed ticking. It is very decorative, and costs practically nothing. In a bedroom, do the swags of eyelet embroidery.

Tricks with paint

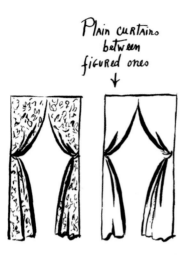

Plain curtains between figured ones

Paper that piano

If you have an enormous living-room and no dining-room, have built a high, four- or five-fold screen. Cover it in flowered chintz, stand it in the middle of the room, and work out from here. On one side, put your serving-table, and use the remaining space for your small tables and chairs. Then curtain the windows in the two halves in different, but complementary, coulours. Keep the carpets alike. On a blank wall, hang a whole collection of those inexpensive wall vases that come from Chinatown. They are bright green and white, and look like vegetables.

While you're down there, take a look at the brilliant paper kites in the form of butterflies. They would make swell decoration, a very chic ceiling, one flying out from each corner and a few scattered around the centre. You'll need a stiff upper lip to get away with that one. Get the butterflies *before* you paint the room, and steal the lovely bold colours from their wings to use on different pieces of furniture. Then when the room is finished, slay the first caller who calls it The Butterfly Room.

In a small bedroom, devoid of promise, paper the walls, ceiling, and doors. Use a plain rug, and plain, flat-textured material in different colours on the furniture…. *Or* paper the ceilings and doors, using a chintz to match the windows, and paint the walls a plain colour…. If your bedroom needs just one extra touch to cheer it up, put down a strip of carpet with bright red roses and vivid green leaves on a white ground, over your plain carpet—like a sidewalk around the three sides of your bed. If you are young and beautiful, put your bed up on a platform about six inches high, paint the platform like a *mille-fleurs* tapestry, in light colours, and hang your bed with embroidered muslin.

Your terrace, if you have one, is a problem, if you want it to be cosy. Regulation garden furniture, I am sure, can *be* cosy, but not look it. Go out into the country and find a second-hand shop—I don't mean an antique shop—but the kind of place that sells to boarding-houses. Invariably the dealer has one or two Edwardian suites he doesn't consider antiques, so they are yours for the price of an old brass bed. It's a nice kind of furniture, with gilt lines and lovely colours in the painting—often with floral or landscape decoration, marble tops on the tables, and quite a lot of architectural nonsense in the design. Obviously for pieces really exposed, you will have to repaint with shiny enamel against the weather. Upholster the chairs and sofas in bright pink or yellow water-proof material; then allow yourself the extra expense of a large canvas sheet to cover the works at night or during a storm. Set the thing up as though it were a living-room, and round it off with rubber plants in the corners. And, in *all* your rooms, put a lot of your own things about—clutter the place up, in a nice way. You want it to be yours, don't you?

If you need one enormous wall decoration, and can't afford a good painted canvas panel, search about for an early twentieth-century scenic curtain used by photographers as the background of the posed victims. Touch up the paint with tempera, and you'll find yourself one of the landed gentry with an urn-guarded estate.

For a small dining-room, use a bright green trellis wallpaper. Put a plaster bust on a bracket on each wall, and paint the busts and brackets in white enamel. Use kitchen furniture painted bright green, with plain magenta seat-pads and curtains, and a dark green fringed cotton rug. Just for effect, salvage from a junk-shop a bulbous, ornate, old-fashioned parlour stove—the taller the better. Lacquer it white, picked out in gold paint, put it in the corner, and keep your extra liquor in it.

For a narrow hall with an uninteresting staircase, paint the walls and floors white. Lay a twenty-seven-inch strip of the brightest crimson carpet you can find, and slip-cover the stair balusters with bright red army cloth or felt, from the rail almost

Overdoor
drapery

Edwardian Terrace

Clutter the
place up

"Ah, the
butterfly
room!"

down to their stair treads. Scallop the bottom edge. On the back wall of your hall, hang a large round or oval Victorian mirror, painted shiny blue-black. Surround it with large black cast-iron hooks to hang your overcoats on, and try a couple of bowler hats for effect. They should be *most* decorative.

To put over a marble Victorian mantel, buy one roll of a beautiful old damask paper. Use it only on the chimney-breast, and paint the rest of the room to match the colour of its background. Set mirrors in squares over your mantel, and drape the mirrors to match the windows in your room. Have a windowbox full of green leaves on the mantel-shelf.

Inexpensive bad idea: Have a simple four-poster bed made, very slender round posts, about nine feet high. Paint it chalk-white, and cut out a Renaissance scalloped valance about one foot deep. Hang cotton tassels between each scallop, stretching it very tight on a frame around the top of the four posts. Dye up enough medium-weight canvas in your favourite colour. Stencil single flowers all over it in white, and let it cover the bed entirely. Even your dogs will have a tough time ruining it.

• • •

*T*he war not only impacted the mood of design but curtailed *decorating resources. As factories converted to wartime production, beautiful fabrics and carpets, both European and domestic, became a rarity. Antiques and art from Europe, long the foundation of fine American design, no longer crossed the ocean. As the situation affected everyone, including readers of* Vogue, *the magazine asked Stacey to advise on decorating within wartime restrictions. Revealing wartime realities and a game spirit of collective sacrifice, Stacey offered extraordinarily down-to-earth advice, far removed from the subtleties of designing with fine furniture and fine art.*

Flats Fixed

How to decorate a three-room flat with sense, nonsense, and small money.... as proposed by George Stacey
(*Vogue*, March 1, 1942)

When Vogue asked me to write this article, my reaction was that there was probably not a single decorating trick left that hadn't already been done. I still feel fairly sure of this. However, I present the following *morceaux* in all good faith and innocence.

It's my theory that tricks in decorating are rather a product of the post-depression. Before that, quality was the key-note. And pretty nice some of it was, and pretty nice it will be, if we can ever get back to it. Meanwhile, though, through the tricks we lose the stuffiness of an overdone period job, and we gain, if you will permit, charm.

Suppose that you have a three-room flat, and as they say, no money. First you come into a small, square hall, and how lucky you are if it *is* square. The existing floor is, of course, bright yellow wood, so you cover it with a plain, bright carpet. Or could you have though that one out for yourself?

Then, as you have NO money, you trek over to the nearest hardware shop. You buy one or, if there is enough space, two tall, thin, corrugated garbage-cans. These go under the brush, all-white or any colour that suits your famous and brilliant carpet. Next, with quite a lot of trouble and a steady hand, pick out the corrugations in black. Right away if you are at all enthusiastic by Nature or Martinis, these ugly pieces will look like the nether end of a fine Doric column. Turn them upside down, now, and use them for pedestals. Add a couple of inexpensive plaster busts. Or large-scale dark green plants. *En fin*, your hall.

Leaving the hall, as by now you will be more than happy to do, we come to the living-room. It has the same yellow floor. This is the big expense. Cover it all up. Paint it, if you normally leave your shoes outside and also don't mind being sued by the building company. Or put down a plain, neutral linoleum and use small Peruvian mats in intense colours. But best of all, carpet it. Perhaps, an inexpensive strip carpet in two or three alternate colors, like a great striped banner.

Paint the walls white, with or without a coloured ceiling. Hang white army cloth at the windows. It's my idea of inexpensive perfection—sun-fast, washable, hangs beautifully. Line each curtain with a different coloured sateen, tied up, of course, with your rug colours. At night, the white is continuous around the room. But when the daylight comes through, each window stands for its own colourful self. Use old-fashioned wicker furniture. Spray the large pieces white, the smaller ones in different colours, with upholstery to match.

Use one corner of the room for dining. Get that little man around the corner to build in two six-foot banquettes at right angles to each other. Salvage from your family's linen closet any large old damask table-cloths you can find. Dye them a wonderful colour; cover the banquettes with them. Put one on the wonderful table that your little man will also build, in unfinished wood—trestle-type to follow the line of the banquettes. To make the table really practical, put glass over the damask.

Opposite the banquettes stand little gilt ballroom chairs. Or, if your friends are the weighty kind, try reproduction ladderbacks, sprayed in clear, bright colours. Use masses of your pet clippings, photographs, maps, mounted on bright-coloured mats. Frame them in simple wood mouldings, dipped in coloured plaster. Hang them all over the place.

Now to the bedroom. For your floor covering use rag rugs, unbelievably inexpensive, in two or three bright colours, squares or plaids. Hang the entire room in, again, army cloth. It comes in very fine colours—though how long it can be obtained for decorating purposes, I don't know. Your curtains become part of the wall. Your beds are springs-and-mattresses on shorts legs. Cover them in the army cloth. Then, for your one splash, make a terrific swoop of butterfly chintz, clear up to the ceiling, back of the beds.

Buy the largest unpainted chest of drawers you can find and cover it in a wonderful wall-paper. Have small bamboo chairs with coloured linen covers and multicoloured buttons.

The bath could be entirely covered with a synthetic basketweave painted any colour you feel for. If the tub looks like the tonneau of a 1918 Rolls, you've achieved something.

In 1964, Stacey's work was included in the design classic The Finest Rooms by America's Great Decorators. *Although the charming accompanying essay affirms the tenets of Stacey's work and captures Stacey's voice, according to close friends, it was most certainly not the direct product of Stacey's pen (and sometimes sacrifices fact to storytelling).*

Cellar Sweeping Was Not for Me

(The Finest Rooms by America's Great Decorators, edited by Katharine Tweed. Viking, 1964.)

It might be of interest to the reader, and also possibly of help to him if he aspires to be a decorator, if I start off by describing the beginning, and some of the more amusing aspects, of my own experience in the field.

After graduating, but only just, from the Parsons School of Design and after spending two summers in Paris, and, I fear a good deal of time in between Stratford, Connecticut, at the age of nineteen I arrived at last at the moment of truth, when a job became something of paramount importance.

Somehow the school had managed to imbue in one the feeling that a decorator is a pretty important person—which is just as well when you are looking for work. During an eight-day voyage from Paris back to New York, I made up my mind that the one person I wanted to work for was Miss Rose Cumming, whose great flair for color and materials was established even then and remains undimmed today. No one who has seen or talked to Miss Cumming could manage, by any trick of the imagination, to think of her as "the girl next door," and by the time I actually arrived in her presence I needed a drink to bolster my rapidly collapsing ego. For some reason, and I suspect it was a mixture of kindness and pity, I was hired and told to report the next morning at her shop, which was then located on Madison Avenue in the fifties. All set to start right in on forty-foot-square Louis XV masterpieces of elegance, I was instead handed a broom and told to sweep the cellar. This task I performed with diligence all day long, and, not having much humor about it at the time, I decided that cellar-sweeping was not for me. Little could I have anticipated that at the end of the Great Depression in the early thirties I would find myself a window dresser in a Philadelphia department store, my special field "kitchen equipment." Miss Cumming had recognized my forte at once.

From these experiences in my early working life I learned a great deal about the business of day-to-day living and working side by side with many different types of workmen which later made it easier for me to understand both my clients and the people of diverse skills who actually carried out the work.

And so it was that several years later through greater experience I was to amend my original estimate of the importance of a decorator, for I knew now that a decorator places somewhere after a psychoanalyst and a plumber—both who are rather more important in a crisis, although perhaps neither a psychoanalyst nor a plumber could produce an attractive interior, even in a crisis.

Skipping now to the post-Depression years, I was eventually offered a job in New York, and it was then that I really got started as a decorator, thanks to one person whose untiring help in finding clients for me resulted in a long and happy career. Without that help I doubt if it could ever have happened. As with any life, the outcome is generally due to a rare chance one is given; after that is up to you.

I am sure that every decorator will agree with me that one of the first and most important things in this profession is to come to know and understand one's clients. This is the analyst side of it. One must know their interests and create as best one can a background in which they both look and feel their best and where their individual interests can best be reflected. One never need worry about expressing oneself; this can be left to the time when a client comes along who really has no interest in decorating: then one can really let oneself go. I am happy to be able to say that I have had very few clients who were uninterested in their houses, so I have not been put to the alternative test, and just as well—although it has been possible for me to work out this urge in one swoop as I was able to acquire a hundred-room Louis XIII château in France and in my spare time to decorate room after room at my own leisure.

Although it is important to do a job which looks as though a decorator had had very little to do with it—as though the room or house had already existed for some time—it is equally important to give the client the chance to take some measure of credit for his own very vital part in the creation of the whole, which certainly is his due. After all, you are in it as a business as well as because it is something you love doing, and not in order to collect pretty phrases.

One of the requisites of a competent decorator is real knowledge of period furniture of any country. It is, in general, a fairly complicated study involving research, comparisons, and a liking for both art and history. With this knowledge, and with a knowledge of color, any young decorator is, I feel sure, well on his way.

In answer to the questions most often put to me about decorating, I would say the following. My favorite classic styles are eighteenth-century French, Italian, and English—in that order. I prefer painted French and Italian furniture to plain wood, and simple rather than elaborate design. I definitely believe in mixing different styles of furniture both in a house and in a room. One of the most common errors people make in decorating is trying to make a room perfect in all the details of a single given period, which inevitably results in a stiff and impersonal back-ground. I am also frequently asked about color schemes suitable for specific rooms, wall-to-wall carpeting, and whether free-standing lamps should or should not all be arranged so that the illumination is at the same height in a room. My answers are: any color scheme in any room is permissible and acceptable provided it suits the owner of the house or apartment; in small, very cut up areas wall-to-wall carpeting makes sense because it tends to minimize angles and to give a feeling of greater space; and free-standing lamps should be at approximately the same height in order to relieve an excess of conflicting shadows.

The question of what pictures to have, and where and how to hang them, seems to arise with persistent urgency. If a person is a collector, or has a good number of original paintings, there is no problem except as to how and where to hang them. They surely need not to be hung according to any rigid rule such as keeping the frames level either at the top or at the bottom; this is a matter for individual preference and taste and may depend on how the pictures relate in color, shape, and style and the position in the room they are to occupy. As to where they should be hung, I prefer to hang them in groups rather than spread them around the room, provided the slide rule isn't used to determine their position. The individual eye should be the invisible "instinctive" slide rule. But if there are no original paintings, and the budget is limited, instead of using reproductions of good paintings I suggest purely decorative ones, or old paintings which are handsome or pretty but of little intrinsic value.

Floors are another important problem in houses and apartments alike. Personally, from the standpoint of beauty, I prefer *parquet de Versailles*, and then herringbone, or carlage.

When asked what I consider to be the most interesting and challenging decorating job I have ever done, I unhesitatingly reply, because it happens to be true: furnishing an old converted three-masted Spanish fruit schooner! And to the frequently asked question as to what originally prompted me to enter the field of decorating, my answer is of the simplest: curiosity. I would like to add—for the benefit and encouragement of young people who are thinking of entering the field—it has been wonderfully satisfied!

Bibliography

Abramson, Rudy. *Spanning the Century: The Life of W. Averell Harriman 1891–1986.* New York: William Morrow and Company, 1992.

Baldwin, Billy, with Michael Gardine. *Billy Baldwin: An Autobiography.* New York: Little, Brown: 1985.

Barlow, Susan. "The Cheney Silk Mills." Manchester Historical Society.

Barrows, Stanley, interview conducted by Martica Swann for the Kellen Design Archives at Parsons School of Design, February 10, 1994.

Bartlett, Apple Parish, and Susan Bartlett Crater. *Sister: The Life of Legendary American Interior Decorator Mrs. Henry Parish II.* New York: Saint Martin's Press, 2000.

Brown, Erica. *Sixty Years of Interior Design: The World of McMillen.* New York: Viking Press, 1982.

Calhoun, John D., and Lewis G. Knapp. *Stratford.* Charleston, South Carolina: Arcadia Publishing, 1999.

Christie's (Monaco) *Collection de m. Henry Clarke, Vendue au Profit de l'institut Pasteur,* sale date 20 June 1998.

Columbia, David Patrick. "New York Social Diary," July 30, 2010.

Columbia, David Patrick. "New York Social Diary," January 20, 2011.

De Wolfe, Elsie. *The House in Good Taste.* (First published in 1913 by the Century Co.) New York: Rizzoli, 2004.

Diliberto, Gioia. *Debutante: The Story of Brenda Frazier.* New York: Knopf, 1987.

Duchin, Peter. *Ghost of a Chance.* New York: Random House, 1996.

Duke, Anthony Drexel, with Richard Firstman. *Uncharted Course: The Voyage of My Life.* Northport, New York: Bayview Press, 2007.

Dwight, Eleanor. *Diana Vreeland.* New York: William Morrow, 2002.

Esten, John. *Diana Vreeland: Bazaar Years.* New York: Universe, 2001.

Gardner, Ava. *Ava: My Story.* New York: Bantam Books, 1990.

Grafton, David. *The Sisters: The Lives and Times of the Fabulous Cushing Sisters.* New York: Villard Books, 1992.

Hampton, Mark. *Legendary Decorators of the Twentieth Century.* New York: Doubleday, 1992.

Haslam, Nicholas. *Redeeming Features.* New York: Knopf, 2009.

Hillairet, Jacques. *Connaissance du Vieux Paris.* Paris: Editions Princesse, 1954.

Kahn Jr., E.J. *Jock: The Life and Times of John Hay Whitney.* New York: Doubleday, 1981.

Katz, Jonathan Ned. "John William Sterling and James Orville Bloss, 1870–1918." http://www.outhistory.org

Kaufmann Jr., Edgar. *Fallingwater: A Frank Lloyd Wright Country House.* New York: Abbeville Press, 1986.

Kavaler, Lucy. *The Astors.* New York: Dodd, Mead and Company, 1966.

Knapp, Lewis G. *In Pursuit of Paradise: History of the Town of Stratford, Connecticut.* Canaan, New Hampshire: Phoenix, 1989.

Kornbluth, Jesse. "The Empress of Clothes." *New York Magazine,* November 29, 1982, 30–36.

Lamont, Thomas W. *Henry P. Davison: The Record of a Useful Life.* New York: Harper & Bros., 1933.

Leigh, Wendy. *True Grace: The Life and Times of an American Princess.* New York: Saint Martin's Press, 2007.

Lewis, Adam. *Van Day Truex: The Man Who Defined Twentieth-Century Taste and Style.* New York: Viking Studio, 2001.

Lewis, Adam. *Albert Hadley: The Story of America's Preeminent Interior Designer.* New York: Rizzoli, 2004.

Metcalf, Pauline C. *Syrie Maugham: Staging Glamorous Interiors.* New York: Acanthus Press, 2010.

Pahlmann, William. *The Pahlmann Book of Interior Design.* New York: Viking, 1968.

"Peacock Point." http://www.oldlongisland.com

Pool, Mary Jane, editor. *20th Century Decorating, Architecture & Gardens: 80 Years of Ideas and Pleasure from House & Garden.* New York: Holt, Rinehart and Winston, 1980.

Quine, Judith Balaban. *The Bridesmaids: Grace Kelly, Princess of Monaco, and Six Intimate Friends.* New York: Grove Press, 1989.

Richardson, John. *Sacred Monsters, Sacred Masters.* New York: Random House, 2001.

Roosevelt, Theodore. *The Autobiography of Theodore Roosevelt.* New York: Scribner's, 1913.

Rowlands, Penelope. *A Dash of Daring: Carmel Snow and Her Life in Fashion, Art, and Letters.* New York: Atria, 2005.

Sartre, Josiane. *Châteaux Brique et Pierre en France.* Paris: Nouvelles Editions Latines, 1981.

Server, Lee. *Ava Gardner.* New York: Saint Martin's Press, 2006.

Smith, Sally Bedell. *In All His Glory: The Life of William S. Paley, The Legendary Tycoon and His Brilliant Circle.* New York: Simon and Schuster, 1990.

Smith, Sally Bedell. *Reflected Glory: The Life of Pamela Churchill Harriman.* New York: Simon and Schuster, 1996.

Snow, Carmel, with Mary Louise Aswell. *The World of Carmel Snow.* New York: McGraw-Hill, 1962.

Sotheby's. *Property from the Estate of Diana D. Vreeland,* sale date April 19, 1990.

Spoto, Donald. *High Society: The Life of Grace Kelly.* New York: Harmony Books, 2009.

Tuchman, Barbara. *The Guns of August.* New York: Macmillan Publishing Company, 1962.

Tuchman, Barbara. *The Proud Tower.* New York: Macmillan Publishing Company, 1966.

Tweed, Katharine, editor. *The Finest Rooms by America's Great Decorators.* New York: Viking Press, 1964.

Van Nes, Mary F. *Into the Wind.* Philadelphia and New York: J. B. Lippincott Company, 1957.

Vreeland, Diana. *D.V.* New York: Knopf, 1984.

White, Norval, and Elliot Willensky. *AIA Guide to New York City.* New York: Three Rivers Press, 2000.

Wharton, Edith, and Ogden Codman Jr. *The Decoration of Houses.* New York: W. W. Norton & Company, 1978.

Wortman, Marc. *The Millionaires' Unit.* New York: Public Affairs, 2006.

Endnotes

CHAPTER ONE

Page 15: The Bayeux Tapestry: Musset, Lucien. *The Bayeux Tapestry*. Paris: Editions Zodiaque, 2002 (English translation: Woodbridge: The Boydell Press, 2005); page 248.

Page 15: Count delivered coup de grâce: Morilllo, Stephen. *The Battle of Hastings: Sources and Interpretation*. Woodbridge: Boydell Press, 1996; page 50.

Page 15: Later maneuvering: Hicks, Carola. *The Bayeux Tapestry: Life Story of a Masterpiece*. London: Chatto and Windus, 2006; page 27.

Page 15: Count's crest depicted accurately: Musset, *The Bayeux Tapestry*, page 248.

Page 16: Tapestry commissioned to regain king's favor: Hicks, *The Bayeux Tapestry: Life Story of a Masterpiece,* page 26.

Page 16: Connecticut drew on Sheffield for labor: Sutherland, John F., *Connecticut's Heritage Gateway,* Manchester Community College, www.ctheritage.org (retrieved October 7, 2011).

Page 17: Ann Stacy and infant arrived: Passenger rolls of the *Garrick,* arriving in New York City on September 12, 1849, show an Ann Stacy, born in 1819, age 30, traveling alone, with one child, John "born at sea." Source: Ancestry.com.

Page 17: John Stacy became a cutler: The 1870 U.S. Census shows a James Stacy, age 52, born in England, a battery polisher; with Ann Stacy, age 51, in Southington, Connecticut. The household also includes John, a laborer "no longer attending school."

Page 17: George's father, Alford Stacy, born in 1880: The 1880 U.S. Census shows John Stacy living in Southington, Connecticut, with his wife, Eliza; the listing includes one child, Alfred, 7 months old.

Page 17: Mrs. Astor called to obtain an invitation for her daughter: Kavaler, Lucy. *The Astors.* New York: Dodd, Mead and Company, 1966. Reprinted Lincoln, Nebraska: Authors Guild Backinprint.com; page 126.

Page 17: Breaking up estates became common in Europe: *The Art Journal.* London: Virtue and Co., Ltd., 1896; page 2.

Page 17: J. P. Morgan antiques collector: "Patron of the Modern," *The Magazine Antiques;* November 2004, volume 166.

Page 17: Ostentatious taste: Kavaler, *The Astors*, page 115.

Page 17: Description of Marble House ballroom: Preservation Society of Newport, http://meetings.newportmansions.org/pdfs/SS_MarbleHouse.pdf (retrieved July 30, 2011).

Page 20: Description of Stratford: *The Journal of the Redman, Okenuck Tribe No. 49* (The local chapter of the Okenucks, a fraternal organization, printed a commemorative history of Stanford 1639–1911). Pages 27–31.

Page 20: Alford Stacey employed as a clerk: Stratford Town Record, 1899.

Page 20: Description of Stratford: *The Journal of the Redman, Okenuck Tribe No. 49,* pages 27–31.

Page 20: Alford Stacey hoped to become an engineer: He listed this as his occupation on George Stacey's birth certificate.

Page 20: Trolley line connected Bridgeport to Stratford: Knapp, Lewis G. *In Pursuit of Paradise: History of the Town of Stratford, Connecticut.* Canaan, New Hampshire: Phoenix, 1989.

Page 20: Marriage: Stratford Town Hall records confirm the marriage.

Page 20: Belle Bennett Morehouse's father was a civil engineer: The 1900 U.S. Census lists William C. Morehouse as a civil engineer.

Page 20: Both members of the church: Alford Stacey appears in the records of the Christ Episcopal Church in Stratford as sponsoring a baptism.

Page 20: Morehouse family has family burial plot with granite obelisk: The family burial plot is in Union Cemetery in Stratford.

Page 20: Strained relationship with family: A visit to Union Cemetery, Stratford, Connecticut, shows that Belle Stacey chose to be buried outside of her family plot, with her husband and friends; she also opted to use her mother's maiden name rather than her own maiden name, Morehouse, as her middle name when married.

Page 21: William Morehouse became town engineer: 1930 U.S. Census.

Page 21: Alford Stacey employment history: References were drawn from Stratford Town Records, 1899, 1902, 1916, 1919, and 1928 and 1920 U.S. Census.

Page 21: Masonic order member: Alford Stacey's few assets on his death included three $100 ten-year notes of the Masonic Temple Association, dated July 1, 1927.

Pages 21-22: Information about Stacey's high school career: 1917 and 1918 editions of the Stratford High School *Clarion.*

Page 22: Friends knew little about Stacey's mother: Interview with Anne Cheney Zinsser, March 1, 2011.

Page 22: Stacey spoke about a house he loved to draw even later in life: Hampton, Mark. *Legendary Decorators of the Twentieth Century.* New York: Doubleday, 1992; page 187.

Page 22: Few graduates left Stratford: Stratford High School *Clarion,* Volume 5, Number 1, November 1917 and Volume 5, Number 5, Commencement 1918, show few departures.

Page 22: Violet Kutcher new to the school: English teacher Violet Kutcher appears on the city payroll in 1917 and 1918.

Page 22: Application process and Yale myth: Hampton, *Legendary Decorators of the Twentieth Century,* page 187.

Page 26: Peacock Point: Wortman, Marc. *The Millionaires' Unit.* New York: Public Affairs, 2006; page 40.

Page 26: Walker and Gillette hired: http://www.oldlongisland.com/2009/09/peacock-point.html (accessed September 29, 2011).

Page 26: Parke-Bernet Building: White, Norval and Elliot Willensky. *AIA Guide to New York City.* New York: Three River Press, 2000; page 298.

Page 26: Fuller Building: White and Willensky, *AIA Guide to New York City,* page 413.

Page 26: Duveen brothers assembled art collection: Interview with Anne Cheney Zinsser, March 1, 2011.

Page 26: Odom was known as "Mr. Taste": Richardson, John. *Sacred Monsters, Sacred Masters.* New York: Random House, 2001; page 66.

Page 26: Odom toured France and Italy every summer until war broke out: "The Influence of William Odom," *House & Garden,* October 1946, pages 88-93.

Page 26: Odom's work still the go-to work on Italian antiques: Stanley Barrows interview, Kellen Design Archives at Parsons The New School for Design, page 34.

Page 27: "His palace fabrics": "Sharp Contrast," *House & Garden,* September 1945, page 73.

CHAPTER TWO

Page 29: Early Parsons staff: New York School of Fine and Applied Arts catalogue, 1919–1920; Kellen Design Archives/Parsons The New School for Design.

Page 30: Early Parsons history: Interview with Stanley Barrows by Martica Sawin, on or about February 10, 1994.

Page 30: "Chic is emphatically necessary": Memo "Qualities for Successful Teaching" found in Francis J. Geck Papers (Geck taught at the Paris Ateliers from 1924-1927), Kellen Design Archives/Parsons The New School for Design.

Page 30: Placement of drawing tools: Interview with Stanley Barrows by Martica Sawin, on or about February 10, 1994.

Page 30: Odom "could not place a book on a table so that it did not look special": Lewis, Adam. *Van Day Truex: The Man Who Defined Twentieth-Century Taste and Style.* New York: Viking Studio, 2001; page 35.

Page 30: Paris Summer School of Architecture and Decoration catalog 1920–1921, page 23; Kellen Design Archives/Parsons The New School for Design.

Page 30: Studying in Paris: Interview with Stanley Barrows by Martica Sawin, on or about February 10, 1994.

Page 30: The greatest value of the program: Francis Geck papers, "Special Summer Session, General Schedule"; Kellen Design Archives/Parsons The New School for Design.

Page 30: Students went to workrooms and antique dealers: From Francis J. Geck Papers Kellen Design Archives/Parsons The New School for Design, measuring is described as "a key to learning the exact relationship to all parts."

Page 30: Students went on trips to the country: "Special Summer Session, General Schedule" (1926); Francis J. Geck Papers, Kellen Design Archives/Parsons The New School for Design.

Pages 30-31 Students visited Versailles and Fontainebleau: "General Suggestions for Visiting on Free Afternoons and After School Hours." Francis J. Geck Papers, Kellen Design Archives/Parsons The New School for Design.

Page 31: Students explored Paris: Interview with Stanley Barrows by Martica Sawin, on or about February 10, 1994.

Page 31: Odom encouraged students to touch work: Interview with Stanley Barrows by Martica Sawin, on or about February 10, 1994.

Page 31: Impressive school patrons: Catalog for Summer Session in France, 1921, Patrons and Patronesses, page 27; Kellen Design Archives/Parsons The New School for Design.

Page 31: "Insure entrance into chateaux and famous private houses not generally accessible to the public": Paris Summer School of Architecture and Decoration, 1920–1921, page 25; Kellen Design Archives/Parsons The New School for Design

Page 32: "Promenade lectures": Francis Geck papers, "Special Summer Session, General Schedule"; Kellen Design Archives/Parsons The New School for Design.

Page 32: Intention for relocating to Hôtel de Chaulnes: Interview with Stanley Barrows by Martica Sawin, on or about February 10, 1994.

Page 32: Stacey developed bond with one instructor: Interview with Anne Cheney Zinsser, March 1, 2011.

Page 33: Odom redecorated hotel suite: *House & Garden,* August 1933, pages 14-15.

Page 34: Odom offered scholarship on the spot: Hampton, *Legendary Decorators of the Twentieth Century,* page 188.

Page 34: Stacey competed in antiques searches: Interview with Betty (Mrs. H. Virgil) Sherrill, December 13, 2011.

Page 34: Odom's style: "The Influence of William Odom," *House & Garden,* October 1946, pages 88-93.

Page 34: Odom's glass collection in the Musée des Arts Décoratifs: "The Influence of William Odom," *House & Garden,* October 1946, pages 88–93.

Page 34:Odom insisted on classes at the Hôtel des Chaulnes: Interview with Stanley Barrows by Martica Sawin, on or about February 10, 1994.

Page 34: Odom was intensely shy and made money from his antiques business: Interview with Stanley Barrows by Martica Sawin, on or about February 10, 1994.

Page 36: Passport sent to Cooper: Stacey's first passport application, filed on February 6, 1922, was obtained through Ancestry.com, Roll #1826; certificate #116260.

Page 36: Cooper's work: Cooper, Daniel. *Inside Your Home.* New York: Farrar, Strauss, 1946.

Page 36: Cooper founded the American Institute of Interior Designers: Alumni Association File, Kellen Design Archives/Parsons The New School for Design.

Page 36: Stacey's mother visited him in Paris: The year Stacey was studying in Paris, his mother applied for a passport, indicating that Paris was one of her destinations.

CHAPTER THREE

Page 39: Stacey described as Paris decorator: "A Little Portfolio of French Interiors," *House & Garden,* June, 1928, pages 81–82.

Page 39: Country was wealthy, as evidenced by ads for appliances: Pool, Mary Jane, editor. *20th Century Decorating, Architecture and Gardens: 80 Years of Ideas and Pleasure from House & Garden.* New York: Holt, Rinehart, and Winston, 1980; page 78.

Page 40: Ship manifests show Stacey crossed the Atlantic: Ship manifests obtained via Ancestry.com.

Page 40: Van Nes family background: Interview with Hans van Nes Jr., October 11, 2011.

Page 40: Story of van Nes meeting his wife: van Nes, Mary. *Into the Wind.* Philadelphia & New York: J. B. Lippincott Company, pages 12–15.

Page 40: Antiques sold easily in 1920s: Interview with Hans van Nes Jr., October 11, 2011.

Page 40: Odom sold privately to decorators: "The Influence of William Odom on American Taste," *House & Garden,* October 1946, page 93.

Page 40: Address of retail store: Address obtained from ship manifests for Hans van Nes in this period, from Ancestry.com

Page 40: 1929 a banner year: Interview with Hans van Nes Jr., October 11, 2011

Page 40: Photo appeared in *Vogue:* "Aids to the Amenities," *Vogue,* December 15, 1932, page 40.

Page 41: Friendships formed in Paris with Andrew Heiskell, Helen Marshall held in special regard: Interview with Anne Cheney Zinsser, March 1, 2011.

Page 41: Marshall was lighthearted: Interview with Alison de Lima Greene, February 13, 2012.

Page 44: Stacey spoke of Marshall frequently throughout his life: Interview with Anne Cheney Zinsser, January 17, 2013.

Page 44: Industrial-style design took hold in 1925: Pool. *20th Century Decorating, Architecture and Gardens: 80 Years of Ideas and Pleasure from House & Garden,* page 78.

Page 44: "Elephantine and out of proportion": Pool, *20th Century Decorating, Architecture and Gardens: 80 Years of Ideas and Pleasure from House & Garden,* page 80.

Page 45: House designed by John Russell Pope in *House & Garden:* Pool. *20th Century Decorating, Architecture and Gardens: 80 Years of Ideas and Pleasure from House & Garden,* page 94.

Page 45: Elsie de Wolfe used a darker palette: Based on photos of rooms by Elsie de Wolfe in 1924, 1925, and 1926; all published in *House & Garden*: Pool, *20th Century Decorating, Architecture and Gardens: 80 Years of Ideas and Pleasure from House & Garden*, page 100.

Page 45: Stacey maintained the business after the lease on the store was terminated: Interview with Hans van Nes Jr., October 11, 2011.

Page 45: Hans van Nes Jr. took Stacey's address to France: Interview with Hans van Nes Jr., October 11, 2011.

Page 45: Alford Stacey died in 1933: Alford Stacey died intestate in May 1933; probate court filings identified George Stacey then living in Paris, France, as his son and next of kin.

CHAPTER FOUR

Page 47: Stacey wanted only to work for Cumming: Tweed, Katharine, editor. *The Finest Rooms by America's Great Decorators*. New York: Viking Press, 1964, page 117.

Page 47: Odom's impeccable taste: Richardson. *Sacred Monsters, Sacred Masters*, page 68.

Page 48: "Like a bag lady, ferreting through items left on the sidewalk for the trash collector": Interview with Jeremiah Goodman, January 9, 2012.

Page 48: Cumming and Otto Kahn: http://www.newyorksocialdiary.com/node/1903049, July 30, 2010.

Page 48: Cumming sometimes changed her mind about selling items: Hampton, *Legendary Decorators of the Twentieth Century*, page 46.

Page 48: Cumming's eccentricities: Interview with Mario Buatta, July 2, 2011.

Page 48: "And by the time I actually arrived in her presence, I needed a drink to bolster my rapidly collapsing ego": Tweed. *The Finest Rooms by America's Great Decorators*, page 117.

Page 48: Stacey swept the cellar: Tweed. *The Finest Rooms by America's Great Decorators*, page 117.

Page 48: Stacey claimed to have worked for Cumming for a single day: Tweed. *The Finest Rooms by America's Great Decorator*, page 117.

Page 48: Stacey met Mrs. Ward Cheney in Cumming's place of business: All Cheney history and details of Stacey's relationship with the Cheney family supplied by Anne Cheney Zinsser (Mrs. John S. Zinsser Jr.), the daughter of Frances and Ward Cheney, in interviews in the course of 2011.

Page 53: Ward Cheney rowed for Yale: *The New York Times*, April 19, 1922, reported that Cheney had been appointed to the stroke seat in the Yale varsity eight-man boat.

Page 53: Ward Cheney's wide-ranging interests: Interview with Anne Cheney Zinsser, March 1, 2011.

Page 53: Cheney wedding discussed in newspapers: *The New York Herald Tribune*, January 1, 1926.

Page 53: Honeymoon apartment featured in *Town & Country*: The *Town & Country* story was written by Augusta Patterson, with photos by Gladys Muller.

Page 53: In that era, women gave birth at Miss Lippincott's Sanitarium: Rowlands, Penelope. *A Dash of Daring: Carmel Snow and Her Life in Fashion, Art and Letters*. New York: Atria Books, 2005; page 104.

Page 53: Food was delivered from the Colony Restaurant: Snow, Carmel. *The World of Carmel Snow*. New York: McGraw-Hill Book Company, 1961; page 65.

Page 53: Frances Cheney's eccentricities: Interview with Anne Cheney Zinsser, January 6, 2013.

Page 53: Café Society: Kahn, E. J. *Jock: The Life and Times of John Hay Whitney*. Garden City, New York: Doubleday & Company, 1981; page 81.

Page 54: Haslam's memories of Frances Cheney: Haslam, Nicholas. *Redeeming Features*. New York: Alfred A. Knopf, 2009; page 212 and interview with Nicholas Haslam, July 2012.

Pages 54, 58: Cinder block excessively porous: Interview with Mrs. Daniel P. Davison, March 2, 2011.

Page 58: Stevenson designed East River Drive: *The New York Times*, September 12, 1984, "Harvey Stevenson, 89, Architect who Helped Design FDR Drive" by Joan Cook, Section D, page 20.

Page 58: Stevenson designed World's Fair Administration Building: *The New York Times*, May 15, 1988, "Streetscapes" by Christopher Gray.

Page 58: Cumming assigned Cheney to Stacey: Interview with Anne Cheney Zinsser, March 1, 2011.

Page 58: Stacey's use of mandarin figure attracted Cheney's attention: Interview with Anne Cheney Zinsser, March 1, 2011.

Page 58: Cheney followed Stacey when he moved to Taylor and Low: In fact, coverage of the Cheney house in *House & Garden*, February 1936, pages 36–37, refers to furniture by Stacey, design by Taylor and Low, indicating some ambiguity of Stacey's employment; also, interview with Anne Cheney Zinsser, March 1, 2011.

Page 60: "Light is everything. Light is what you see. Light is all you see": Interview with Hans van Nes Jr. October 11, 2011.

Page 60: "Beautiful baroque drawing room, hung with chartreuse-yellow taffeta curtains and with pale chocolate colored walls": *Vogue*, April 15, 1934, "Background for Beauty," page 44.

Page 61: "Following the Mohammedan routine, shoes are removed before entering": *Town & Country*, August 1936, "Revolutionary Cottage," pages 61–63.

Page 61: Hadley noted that tall candles were a Stacey constant: Interview with Albert Hadley, June 27, 2011.

Page 61: Design of Fallingwater: Kauffman, Edgar Jr. *Fallingwater: A Frank Lloyd Wright Country House*. New York: Abbeville Press, 1986. Pages 39–46 give the chronology of the move in to Fallingwater.

Page 61: Eleanor Brown designed her own apartment: Brown, Erica. *Sixty Years of Interior Design: The World of McMillen*. New York: Viking Press, 1982; pages 49–50. (Mrs. Brown's maxim was "If you get it right the first time, there is no need to change." Her 1930s dining room was effectively unchanged for fifty years.)

Page 61: Berlin Exposition: Pool. *20th Century Decorating, Architecture and Gardens: 80 Years of Ideas and Pleasure from House & Garden*, page 118.

Page 63: Younger members of the Davison family thought Stacey was a relative: Interview with Harry Davison, June 17, 2011.

Page 63: Ward Cheney and Stacey spent time together in Europe: Interview with Anne Cheney Zinsser, March 1, 2011.

Page 63: Stacey never discussed his projects: Interview with James Davison, May 29, 2011.

Page 63: Alice Gates appeared on best dressed lists: Interview with Anne Cheney Zinsser, January 6, 2013.

Page 63: Alice Gates was as well regarded as her sister: Interview with Anne Cheney Zinsser, March 1, 2011.

Page 63: Stacey expanded client roster with high-profile names: *Vogue*, March 1, 1942, "And What's More…"

Page 63: "Miss Helen Marshall has a strong sense of color used decoratively. She conveys an acute sense of atmosphere….she interprets with a scientific precision certain articles that hold the spectator's interest, since their appeal to the eye is equally as strong as their appeal to the mind": *Apollo* magazine, April 1934, pages 222–223.

Page 63: Marshalls' marriage and background: Interview with Frederic Papert, February 18, 2012.

Page 63: Stacey sought professional help to deal with Marshall's marriage: Taken from Stacey's recorded comments during the proceedings of the Army Retiring Board, July 1, 1943.

CHAPTER FIVE

Page 65: Vreeland returned to New York: Dwight, Eleanor. *Diana Vreeland*. New York: William Morrow, 2002; page 43.

Page 65: Vreeland at court: Vreeland, Diana. *D.V.* New York: Alfred A. Knopf, 1984; page 63.

Page 65: Vreeland cut out magazine articles: Dwight. *Diana Vreeland*, page 40.

Page 65: Vreeland changed pronunciation of her name: Dwight. *Diana Vreeland*, page 43.

Page 65: Vreeland's life in London: Dwight. *Diana Vreeland*, page 32.

Page 65: Daisy Fellowes at *Harper's Bazaar*: Esten, John. *Diana Vreeland: Bazaar Years*. New York: Universe, 2001; page 12.

Page 65: Discovery of Vreeland: Vreeland. *D.V.*, page 89.

Page 65: Sandal commissioned: Vreeland. *D.V.*, page 110.

Page 66: Vreeland's Palm Beach attire: *Town & Country*, February 1937. (Brightly colored contrasting zippers were the innovation of Elsa Schiaparelli, one of Vreeland's preferred designers in the 1930s.)

Page 66: Vreeland's comment on the bikini: Dwight. *Diana Vreeland*, page 43.

Page 66: Vreeland met Elsie de Wolfe in 1931: Dwight. *Diana Vreeland*, page 36. Vreeland. *D.V.*, page 44.

Page 66: Stacey's design for Vreeland: Sotheby's. *Property from the Estate of Diana D. Vreeland*, Thursday April 19, 1990, New York. Foreword, "D.V.: The Last Great Romantic" by Bill Blass.

Page 66: Description of Stacey's palette: Hampton. *Legendary Decorators of the Twentieth Century*, page 184.

Page 66: "All my life I've pursued the perfect red...the best red is...the color of a child's cap in any Renaissance portrait": Vreeland. *D.V.*, page 103.

Pages 66-67 "Realize, realize the return of black, and black and white, in decoration. It is of tremendous importance": Esten. *Diana Vreeland Bazaar Years*, page 70.

Page 67: Edward Warburg a Stacey client: *Vogue*, March 1, 1942, "And What's More..."

Page 67: "Blackamoors all over the place...and paper-white narcissus in salad bowls": *New York Magazine*, November 29, 1982, "The Empress of Clothes" by Jesse Kornbluth, page 33.

Page 67: Details including dimensions of Park Avenue apartment contents: Sotheby's. *Property from the Estate of Diana D. Vreeland*, Thursday, April 19, 1990, New York. Lots 43 and 103.

Page 67: "A practicality of clean lines, fresh ideas, and relentless professionalism": Sotheby's. *Property from the Estate of Diana D. Vreeland*, Thursday April 19, 1990, New York. Foreword, "D.V.: The Last Great Romantic" by Bill Blass.

Page 67: "Threw ropes of costume jewelry onto everything in this wonderful way": Description of Coco Chanel's style is excerpted from Vreeland's Acoustiguide for the Costume Institute exhibit at the Metropolitan Museum of Art, "The 10's, the 20's, The 30's: inventive clothes from 1909-1939"

Pages 67, 69: Blackamoors named as style trend in the magazine: *Harper's Bazaar*, March 1938, "The New Fantastic."

Page 69: Blackamoors popular in Paris: Vreeland. *D.V.*, page 53.

Page 69: Items were sold as part of 1990 estate sale: Sotheby's. *Property from the Estate of Diana D. Vreeland*, Thursday April 19, 1990, New York.

Page 69: Red mirror curtains: Dwight. *Diana Vreeland*, page 55.

Page 69: "Another pair of blackamoors": Sotheby's. *Property from the Estate of Diana D. Vreeland*, Thursday April 19, 1990, New York. Lot 116.

Page 69: Mirrors: Sotheby's. *Property from the Estate of Diana D. Vreeland*, Thursday April 19, 1990, New York. Lot 100.

Page 69: Brackets: Sotheby's. *Property from the Estate of Diana D. Vreeland*, Thursday April 19, 1990, New York. Lots 83–87.

Page 69: Sconces: Sotheby's. *Property from the Estate of Diana D. Vreeland*, Thursday April 19, 1990, New York. Lot 45.

Page 69: Vreeland noted importance of a mirror: From Diana Vreeland house book notes. Diana Vreeland papers. Manuscripts and Archives Division. The New York Public Library. Astor, Lenox, and Tilden Foundations.

Page 75: "Why Don't You... build in a bunk like Shirley Temple's in *Captain January* with drawers underneath for clothes and toys?": Esten. *Diana Vreeland: Bazaar Years*, page 67. (*Captain January* was released in 1936.)

Page 75: Vreeland's feelings about household management: Dwight. *Diana Vreeland*, page 29. Diana wrote, "I believe in tidy housekeeping, I believe in neatness, I believe in a fresh bed, a clean dressing table. But these are *first* things."

Page 75: Vreeland took detailed notes: Entertaining and household notebooks are found in the Diana Vreeland papers. Manuscripts and Archives Division. The New York Public Library. Astor, Lenox, and Tilden Foundations.

Page 75: "Why Don't You...go to [a] theatrical-material shop, and get fake leopard skin?": Esten. *Diana Vreeland: Bazaar Years*, page 62.

Page 75: Suggestion to use a white fur on a bed: Esten. *Diana Vreeland: Bazaar Years*, page 57.

Page 75: "By far and away the most romantic country house you could ever imagine": Vreeland. *D.V.*, page 81.

Page 75: Frances Cheney collected the work of Jean Schlumberger: Interview with Anne Cheney Zinsser, January 6, 2013.

Page 75: Cyclamen pink ceiling: Dwight. *Diana Vreeland*, page 66.

Pages 75, 78: Shocking pink was Elsa Schiaparelli's signature color: Dwight. *Diana Vreeland*, page 69.

Page 78: Balenciaga colors: Golbin, Pamela. *Balenciaga, Paris*. London: Thames and Hudson, 2006; page 32. (Catalog published to coincide with the exhibition "Balenciaga, Paris" at Les Arts Décoratifs, Musée de la Mode et du Textile, Paris, 2006.)

Page 78: Canopy bed: Vreeland. *D.V.*, page 81.

Pages 78-79: Décor of room: *Harper's Bazaar*, May 1941: "Why Don't You...use *broderie anglaise* antimacassars—threaded with colored ribbons—on the backs and arms of miniature over-stuffed chairs?"

Page 79: Louise Dahl-Wolfe training and reputation: Rowlands. *A Dash of Daring: Carmel Snow and Her Life in Fashion, Art, and Letters*, page 207.

Page 79: *Harper's Bazaar* published Dahl-Wolfe's photographs of Stacey's interiors for Vreeland in three of its issues: "*Harper's Bazaar*, March 15, 1941 pages 66-67; April 1, 1941, pages 64–67; May 1, 1942, pages 38–39.

CHAPTER SIX

Pages 83-84: Information on The Decorators Picture Gallery: Most information on The Decorators Picture Gallery was obtained in gallery record books in the possession of Frances Cheney's family; further information was found in *Vogue*, January 15, 1937, page 94; and *Vogue*, November 1, 1937, page 59.

Page 84: Stacey display at The Decoraters Picture Gallery: "Decorator's Day-Book" *Vogue*, April 1, 1938, page 60.

Page 84: Fifth Avenue apartment: All background on the Fifth Avenue apartment as well as the apartment at 4 East 66th Street was provided by Anne Cheney Zinsser in interviews in 2011 and 2012.

Page 84: Vreeland staged two shoots in the apartment: "Feminine After Five," *Harper's Bazaar*, March 1941, pages 58–59, and "Private Worlds," *Harper's Bazaar*, April 1941, page 63.

Page 84: *Town & Country* story with van Nes photographs: *Town & Country,* February 1941, "The Last of Mrs. Cheney" by Augusta Owen Patterson, page 74.

Page 84: *Vogue* article: "A Place for Beauty," *Vogue,* December 1, 1942, page 114.

Page 89: "A radical in velvet": *Town & Country,* February 1941, "The Last of Mrs. Cheney" by Augusta Owen Patterson, page 74.

Pages 89, 92: Perona noted that New Yorkers liked to look at themselves: Grafton, David. *The Sisters: The Lives and Times of the Fabulous Cushing Sisters.* New York: Villard Books, 1992; page 60.

Page 92: 'Give us O Lord our daily platitude' can never be written about Frances Cheney or her decorator George Stacey": *Town & Country,* February 1941, "The Last of Mrs. Cheney" by Augusta Owen Patterson, page 74.

Page 92: Room could serve as a gym: "A Place for Beauty," *Vogue,* December 1, 1942, page 114.

Page 92: "I have seen the flock paper he is going to use": "A Dish for Decorators"; *The Spur,* March 30, 1938.

Page 92: Frances Elkins also used Victorian items in her designs: *Harper's Bazaar,* April 1939, page 79.

Page 92: "A witty comment on decoration": "Decorator's Day Book," *Vogue,* April 1, 1938, page 60.

CHAPTER SEVEN

Page 95: Billy Baldwin description of Stacey's prominence in the decorating world: Gardine, Michael. *Billy Baldwin: An Autobiography.* New York: Little, Brown & Company, 1985; page 274.

Page 96: Kitty Bache Miller hired Stacey: "And What's More...," *Vogue;* March 1, 1942. (A sketch of the Millers' red and green dining room appears in "The Clue is Color," *Vogue,* April 15, 1945, page 144.)

Page 96: Miller was unhappy: Gardine. *Billy Baldwin: An Autobiography,* page 274.

Page 96: Edward Warburg and Stacey: "And What's More...,"; *Vogue,* March 1, 1942.

Page 96: Edward Warburg's art collection: Pace, Eric. "Arts, Ballet Ally Edward Warburg, 84," *The New York Times,* September 22, 1992.

Page 96: Warburg's cultural connections: Birmingham, Stephen. *Our Crowd.* New York: Harper & Row, 1967; page 384.

Page 96: The William Harknesses were Stacey clients: "And What's More...," *Vogue,* March 1, 1942.

Page 96: Mona Williams: Hampton. *Legendary Decorators of the Twentieth Century,* page 190.

Page 96: Minnie Cushing's salon: Grafton. *The Sisters: The Lives and Times of the Fabulous Cushing Sisters,* page 172.

Page 96: East End Avenue apartment: "The New York Apartment of Commander and Mrs. Vincent Astor," *Vogue,* September 1, 1942; page 55; Kavaler, *The Astors.*

Page 100: Single French item: "The New York Apartment of Commander and Mrs. Vincent Astor," *Vogue,* September 1, 1942, page 54-57.

Page 103: Astor guest bedroom: "Bed, Bath and Beauty," *House & Garden;* January 1948, page 64.

Page 103: Whitneys' taste: Grafton. *The Sisters: The Lives and Times of the Fabulous Cushing Sisters,* page 284.

Page 103: Jock Whitney purchased a Renoir after lunch: Kahn. *Jock: The Life and Times of John Hay Whitney,* page 126.

Page 103: Whitney turned over his yacht: Kahn. *Jock: The Life and Times of John Hay Whitney,* page 148.

Page 103: Betsey Whitney and her daughters appeared in *Vogue:* "Mrs. John Hay Whitney with her daughters, Sara and Kate Roosevelt"; *Vogue,* April 15, 1945, page 59.

Pages 103, 104: *House & Garden* story about Stacey and Minnie Astor: "There is Nothing More Personal than Taste," *House & Garden,* October 1948, page 113.

Page 104: Betsey Whitney invited Stacey to her country house: Interview with James Davison, May 29, 2011.

Page 104: Babe Paley hired Stacey to decorate apartment: Smith, Sally Bedell. *In All His Glory: The Life of William S. Paley, The Legendary Tycoon and His Brilliant Circle.* New York: Simon and Schuster, 1990; page 251.

Page 104: "Riff, Raff, and Ruin": Smith. *In All His Glory: The Life of William S. Paley, The Legendary Tycoon and His Brilliant Circle,* page 251.

Page 104: Stacey's design for Babe Paley's apartment: Smith. *In All His Glory: The Life of William S. Paley, The Legendary Tycoon and His Brilliant Circle,* page 251.

Page 104: Babe Paley's tastes in antiquing: Smith. *In All His Glory: The Life of William S. Paley, The Legendary Tycoon and His Brilliant Circle,* page 251.

Page 104: Babe Paley fond of Louis XVI chairs: Smith. *In All His Glory: The Life of William S. Paley, The Legendary Tycoon and His Brilliant Circle,* Appendix II, page 1.

Page 104: Townsend Martin's relationship to Henry Phipps: *New York Times* obituary April 25, 2010, of Michael Townsend Martin.

Page 104: Martin won Jockey Gold Cup twice: Cravat won the Jockey Club Gold Cup in 1939; Bolingbroke won in 1944; both horses were owned by Townsend B. Martin.

Page 104: Stacey decoration in Martin home: "Mr. and Mrs. Townsend B. Martin's House in Connecticut," *Vogue,* October 15, 1944, pages 118–119.

Page 104: Ward Cheney's military service: Interview with Anne Cheney Zinsser, April 12, 2011.

Page 104: Harriman in London: Abramson, Rudy. *Spanning the Century: The Life of Averell Harriman 1891–1986.* New York: William Morrow and Company, Inc., 1992; pages 275–276 and 298–299.

Page 104: Marie Harriman remained in New York: Smith. *Reflected Glory.* New York: Simon & Schuster, 1996; page 89.

Page 104: "The Disappearing Dining Room": "The Disappearing Dining Room," *Harper's Bazaar,* March 1947, page 211.

Page 108: "It strikes an accord among friends who feel deeply...in a year such as this, gifts of trivia are not in order": "A Bond Between Friends," *Harper's Bazaar,* December 1943, page 49.

Page 108: Artemus Gates's position: Wortman, Marc. *The Millionaires' Unit.* New York: Public Affairs, 2006; pages 298–299.

Page 108: Stanley Mortimer enlisted in the fledgling Navy Air Force: Grafton. *The Sisters: The Lives and Times of the Fabulous Cushing Sisters,* page 62.

Page 110: Stacey's exit from the army: U.S. Army personnel records, Stacey, George Alford file; request #1-9364615005.

Page 110: Frances Cheney's mother invited Stacey to Peacock Point: Letter from Mrs. Henry Davison to George Stacey, May 31, 1943.

Page 111: Frances Cheney lent Stacey squash court: Interview with Anne Cheney Zinsser, April 12, 2011.

Page 111: Squash court on the cover of *House & Garden:* The cover of *House & Garden,* September 1945.

Pages 111, 117 "An enchanting little house...A weekend there with him could not have [been] more fun. The bathroom facilities were slightly odd in that the shower was outside in front of the house; consequently you had the advantage there of showing off to everybody": Gardine. *Billy Baldwin: An Autobiography,* page 275.

Page 117: Stacey rented apartment on East 56th Street: "Rents Apartment in Beekman Place," *The New York Times,* July 17, 1943, page 22.

Page 117: "Timeless and distinguished, very often brilliant, with undefinable chic…a color sense of Renaissance braggadocio"; comfortable space; "an opulent depth": "Sharp Contrast: Undated Decoration, Signature of a Top Flight Decorator," *House & Garden*, September 1945, pages 73–75.

Page 117: "Unbelievable, unhistorical mélange—Chinese, Louis XVI, Empire, Victorian": "Sharp Contrast: Undated Decoration, Signature of a Top Flight Decorator," *House & Garden*, September 1945, pages 73–75.

Page 117: *Celebutante* invented to describe Brenda Frazier: *Oxford English Dictionary* citing the *Nevada State Journal*, April 11, 1939.

Page 117: "Please stop giving the Stork Club free publicity!": Diliberto, Gioia. *Debutante: The Story of Brenda Frazier.* New York: Knopf, 1987; page 185.

CHAPTER EIGHT

Page 121: Billy Baldwin's view of Stacey: Gardine. *Billy Baldwin: An Autobiography*, pages 274–275.

Page 121: "Decorator, stage-set designer, and psychologist": "There is Nothing More Personal than Taste," *House & Garden*, October 1948, page 110.

Page 122: Somerset House: "Bermuda Restoration," *Vogue*, January 1, 1947, pages 112–113.

Pages 122-123: Cheney drawing room: "The Clue is Color," *Vogue*, April 15, 1945, page 145.

Pages 123, 128: Lil Isles painted: Interview with Jill Blanchard, March 5, 2012.

Page 128: Isles' appearance in public without makeup reported in *Vogue*: "St. Moritz: Holiday with Skis," *Vogue*, December 1952.

Page 128: "Breathtakingly attractive—the *most* chic": Interview with Gloria Schiff, March 2, 2012.

Page 128: Isles' dining room: Interview with Jill Blanchard, March 5, 2012; interview with Tina Barney, March 19, 2012.

Page 128: "Colors from an Italian painting in a New York dining room": *House & Garden,* November 1947, page 130.

Pages 128, 130: Description of Isles' apartment: Interview with Philips Isles Jr., March 21, 2012.

Pages 128, 130: Impression Stacey made on the Isles children and love for guest bedroom: Interview with Jill Blanchard, March 2, 2012.

Page 130: Stacey's design for Isles' country home: Interview with Gloria Schiff, March 2, 2012.

Page 130: Children's reaction to country house: Interview with Jill Blanchard, March 2, 2012.

Page 133: Anita Pallenberg and Keith Richards rented Isles' country home: Interview with Geoffrey Isles, December 7, 2012.

Page 133: Pallenberg and wine bottles: Richards, Keith. *Life.* Boston: Little Brown & Company, 2010; page 380.

Page 133: "It was polite and pretty, rather like a nice country club": Smith. *In All His Glory: The Life of William S. Paley, The Legendary Tycoon and His Brilliant Circle*, page 113.

Page 133: Paley had gold dog tag: Smith. *In All His Glory: The Life of William S. Paley, The Legendary Tycoon and His Brilliant Circle*, page 208.

Page 133: Babe Paley sought French antiques: Smith. *In All His Glory: The Life of William S. Paley, The Legendary Tycoon and His Brilliant Circle*, page 330.

Page 133: The resurgence of fine French furniture after World War II is partially explained by the strength of the U.S. dollar in France, and perhaps Stacey's highly visible use of French furniture for his fashionable clients.

Page 133: Babe Paley photographed for *Vogue*: "Mrs. William S. Paley in Her House 'Kiluna Farm,'" *Vogue*, November 1, 1950, pages 114–115.

Page 136: "The most glamorous, black-haired, gardenia-skinned, ruby-lipped debutante who ever wore a strapless dress": David Patrick Columbia. http://www.newyorksocialdiary.com/node/1904978, January 20, 2011.

Page 139: Description of Frazier's house as "a plot of Virginia moved north": "At Meadow Wood Farm"; *Vogue*, September 15, 1947, pages 162–163 and 198.

Page 139: Frazier's parties: Diliberto. *Debutante: The Story of Brenda Frazier*, pages 187–189.

Page 139: Constance Spry florist for Frazier's debutante party: Diliberto. *Debutante: The Story of Brenda Frazier*, page 120.

Page 139: Stacey liked informal floral arrangements: "At Meadow Wood Farm," *Vogue*, September 15, 1947, pages 162–163 and page 198.

Page 139: Mrs. Anthony Drexel Duke photographed for *Vogue*: "Mrs. Anthony Drexel Duke, Living Room," *Vogue*, October 15, 1948, page 111.

Page 144: Furniture in Cheney home: *Town & Country*, February 1945, page 52.

Pages 144, 146: Furniture in Astor home: "There is Nothing More Personal than Taste," *House & Garden*, October 1948, page 110.

Page 146: Stacey went to visit at McMillen: Interview with Mrs. H. Virgil (Betty) Sherrill, December 12, 2011.

Page 146: Stacey would drop in to chat at Thedlow: Conversation with Pauline Metcalf.

Page 146: Stacey kept his hat on: Gardine. *Billy Baldwin: An Autobiography*, pages 274-275.

Page 147: Stacey often used Frederick P. Victoria furniture and dined with the family weekly: Interview with Anthony Victoria, February 1, 2011.

Page 147: "Insecure, pompous and rude, and not exactly attractive": Interview with Jeremiah Goodman, January 9, 2012.

Page 147: Hadley's meeting with Stacey: Interview with Albert Hadley, June 27, 2011.

Page 147: Stacey remained close to Marshall: Interview with Anne Cheney Zinsser, March 1, 2011.

Page 147: Hannath Marshall worked at Ogilvy: Interview with Frederic Papert, February 18, 2012.

Page 147: Stanley Barrows considered Marshall an excellent teacher, particularly of life drawing: Interview with Stanley Barrows by Martica Sawin, on or about February 10, 1994, page 76 of transcript.

CHAPTER NINE

Page 149: Jean-Louis Raynaud alerted Stacey to available Paris apartment in the *hôtel particulier* he owned: Interview with Alain Raynaud, July 19, 2011.

Page 151: Architectural history of I, rue de la Chaise: Hillaret, J. *Connaissance du Vieux Paris*, Paris: Editions Princesse, 1954; page 232.

Page 151: Description of apartment: "Well-Decorated: A Notebook of Ideas," *Vogue*, October 15, 1950, page 90.

Page 151: Stacey's furnishings: Interview with Charles Sevigny, May 29, 2011.

Page 151: Stacey invited to serve as an adviser at Parsons: Lewis. *Van Day Truex: The Man Who Defined Twentieth-Century Taste and Style*, page 158; Gardine. *Billy Baldwin: An Autobiography*, page 275.

Page 151: Stacey insecure around Truex: Interview with Anne Cheney Zinsser, April 11, 2011.

Page 151: Baldwin's description of the relationship between Stacey and Truex: Gardine. *Billy Baldwin: An Autobiography*, page 275.

Page 151: Stacey decorated Blanche Levy's house: "Palm Beach: The Lake Worth House of Dr. and Mrs. Leon Levy," *Vogue*, April 1, 1959, pages 133–134.

Page 151: Stacey benefited from availability of antiques in postwar period: Interview with Anthony Victoria, June 28, 2012.

Page 158: Pieces that Stacey acquired for Levy house still in the family: Interview with Rochelle Levy, January 23, 2012.

Page 158: Grace Kelly was Levy neighbor: Interview with Rochelle Levy, January 23, 2012.

Page 158: Kelly appreciated French furniture: Leigh, Wendy. *True Grace: The Life and Times of an American Princess.* New York: St. Martin's Press, 2007; page 94.

Page 158: Kelly's favorite authors were French: Leigh, Wendy. *True Grace: The Life and Times of an American Princess.* New York: St. Martin's Press, 2007; page 117.

Page 158: Kelly lived in the Manhattan House: Leigh. *True Grace: The Life and Times of an American Princess,* page 40.

Page 158: Kelly had old family furniture in early years: Spoto, Donald. *High Society: The Life of Grace Kelly.* New York: Harmony Books, 2009; page 56.

Page 158: Kelly moved to Fifth Avenue: Spoto. *High Society: The Life of Grace Kelly,* page 192.

Page 158: Kelly's apartment overlooked the Metropolitan Museum of Art: Spoto. *High Society: The Life of Grace Kelly,* page 191.

Page 158: Kelly's living room had French antiques: Quine, Judith Balaban. *The Bridesmaids: Grace Kelly, Princess of Monaco and Six Intimate Friends.* New York: Weidenfield and Nicholson, 2009; page 102.

Page 158: Kelly's apartment had Frederick P. Victoria furniture: Interview with Anthony Victoria, February 1, 2011.

Page 158: Kelly acquired fresh flower arrangements twice a week: Spoto. *High Society: The Life of Grace Kelly,* page 192.

Page 158: Kelly hosted parties: Quine. *The Bridesmaids: Grace Kelly, Princess of Monaco and Six Intimate Friends,* page 110.

Page 161: Kelly remained loyal to Stacey in the face of an offer from Lee Radziwill: Letter from Princess Grace to George Stacey, April 13, 1976.

Page 161: Emilio Terry had previously decorated the apartments: http://courlande.pagesperso-orange.fr/rochecotte.htm (consulted April 14, 2011).

Page 161: Yellow was Princess Grace's favorite color: Quine. *The Bridesmaids: Grace Kelly, Princess of Monaco and Six Intimate Friends,* page 227.

Page 161: Picasso depiction of a king: Leigh. *True Grace: The Life and Times of an American Princess,* page 156.

Page 162: Rita Gam and Thomas Guinzburg married in the room: Quine. *The Bridesmaids: Grace Kelly, Princess of Monaco and Six Intimate Friend,* page 10.

Page 162: Harriman had simple tastes: Duchin, Peter. *Ghost of a Chance.* New York: Random House, 1996; page 89.

Page 162: Description of Stacey design for Harriman residence: Interview with Alida W. Morgan, January 27, 2013.

Page 162: Harriman found working with Stacey easy: Interview with Alida W. Morgan, January 27, 2013.

Page 162: Duchin saw Stacey as good company: Interview with Peter Duchin, February 14, 2013.

Page 162: Harrimans' art collection: "Mrs. Harriman's Famous Art Collection," *Vogue,* February 1, 1944, page 81.

Page 162: Entrance hall to Harrimans' residence: Interview with Alida W. Morgan, January 27, 2013.

Page 164: Stacey suggested purchase to Harriman: Interview with Peter Duchin, February 14, 2013.

Page 164: "Pure Stacey": Interview with Alida W. Morgan, January 27, 2013.

Page 165: Description of Harriman home in Sands Point: Abramson, Rudy. *Spanning the Century: The Life of Averell Harriman 1891–1986.* New York: William Morrow and Company, Inc., 1992; page 73.

Page 165: Description of Harriman home in Sands Point: Duchin. *Ghost of a Chance,* page 89.

Page 165: Description of interiors of Harriman house, including "the most glamorous bedroom in the world!": Interview with Wendy Goodman, November 29, 2012.

Page 165: Description of governor's mansion; "early Halloween": Abramson. *Spanning the Century: The Life of Averell Harriman 1891–1986,* page 521.

Page 165: Minister of the Interior: Interview with Alida W. Morgan, January 27, 2013, interview with Peter Duchin, February 14, 2013.

Page 165: Stacey's work for younger clients: Interview with Mrs. H. Virgil (Betty) Sherrill, December 12, 2011.

Page 166: Stacey leased château: "*Vogue's* Fashions for Living: American Decorator's Plan for a French Chateau," *Vogue,* September 15, 1956, page 156.

Page 166: Stacey leased château in 1956: Hampton. *Legendary Decorators of the Twentieth Century,* page 193.

Page 166: Château built to plans by Cerceau: Sartre, Josiane. *Châteaux en Brique et Pierre en France.* Paris. Nouvelles Editions Latines, 1981; page 137.

Page 166: "Great love": Interview with Albert Hadley, June 24, 2011.

Page 166: Château used as film location: Interview with Anne Cheney Zinsser, April 11, 2011.

Page 166: Stacey's selection of cars: Interview with Alain Raynaud, July 20, 2011.

Page 166: Stacey's relationship with locals: Interview with Anne Cheney Zinsser, April 11, 2011

Page 166: Stacey taken for a priest: Interview with Alain Raynaud, July 20, 2011.

Page 166: Stacey stayed to himself: Interview with Anne Cheney Zinsser, April 11, 2011.

Page 166: Stacey invited Hadley and Baldwin to visit: Interview with Albert Hadley, June 24, 2011.

Page 166: "I know you always stay with the Windsors when you come to France." Gardine. *Billy Baldwin: An Autobiography,* page 275.

Page 166: "All-American aristocrat": *House & Garden,* March 1992, "All American Aristocrat" by Mark Hampton, page 106.

Page 166: *Vogue* published photographs of the château: "*Vogue's* Fashions for Living/American Decorator's Plan for a French Chateau," *Vogue,* September 15, 1956, page 156.

Page 172: Life at La Tourelle: www.metropoleparis.com/1997/70922238/tourelle.html "The End of Heritage in Rochefort," September 22, 1997.

Page 172: Stacey's friendships in France: Interview with Alain Raynaud, July 20, 2011.

Page 172 : Description of Poteau's house: Christie's catalog *Collection de M. Henry Clarke,* sale date 20 June 1998.

Page 172: Henry Clarke's apartment: "Fashions in Living: Pied á Paris—a mansard-roofed attic on the Left Bank," *Vogue,* August 15, 1957, pages 138–139.

Page 172: Marshall exhibited paintings at the Durlacher Brothers gallery: *ARTnews*: Volume 53, March 1954; volume 54, page 42; February 1956, page 52; volume 58, March 1959, page 13.

Page 175: Marshall exhibited paintings at the Whitney Annual: Whitney Annual Exhibition January 12–February 20, 1955. Catalog obtained in the Whitney Museum of American Art Research Library.

Page 175: Marshall exhibited paintings at the Corcoran Biennial: Falk's Exhibition Record, Metropolitan Museum of Art.

Page 175: Marshall exhibited paintings at the Museum of Modern Art: Registrar's office, Museum of Modern Art, August 2, 2011.

Page 175: ARTnews praised Marshall's paintings: ARTnews, February 1956, volume 54, page 52.

Page 175: "Her paintings express intelligence and control. She knows what she wants to do and she finds out how to do it": ARTnews, March 1959, volume 58, page 13.

Page 175: Marshall's lifestyle: After 1953, Helen Marshall became curriculum coordinator for Parsons New York and Paris (Kellen Design Archives, Parsons The New School for Design).

Page 175: James Davison's time in Paris: Interview with James Davison, May 29, 2011.

Page 175: Stacey's presumed romantic partner, Billy: Interview with James Davison, May 29, 2011.

CHAPTER TEN

Page 177: Attempt to make Parsons into a school of environmental design: Lewis. Van Day Truex: The Man Who Defined Twentieth-Century Taste and Style, page 178.

Page 179: Ava Gardner and Juan Perón were neighbors: Gardner, Ava. Ava: My Story. New York, Bantam Books, 1990; page 273.

Page 179: Stacey's decoration of Gardner's apartment: Tweed. The Finest Rooms by America's Great Decorators, page 129.

Page 179: Gardner's feeling about her father: Gardner. Ava: My Story, pages 16–19.

Page 179: Gardner liked to run in Stacey's fields: Interview with Doug Wright, March 16, 2011.

Page 179: "And right now, there is an old man somewhere in Spain boasting at the taberna of his night with Ava Gardner": Interview with Anne Cheney Zinsser, March 1, 2011.

Page 179: "Expecting and wanting to be paid": Interview with Jess Morgan, May 20, 2011.

Page 179: Stacey was discreet about Gardner: Interview with Harry Davison, June 17, 2011.

Page 179: Stacey arranged film mementos at Roc Agel: Leigh. True Grace: The Life and Times of an American Princess, page 159.

Page 182: "I am off to Paris by road driving this silly little car of mine: the Rolls Royce! (The ash tray is already full!)": Letter from Prince Rainier, delivered to Stacey by hand at the Hotel Bristol, Monte Carlo, dated 7th October (no year).

Page 182: Stacey decorated apartment in Paris for Princess Grace and her family: Leigh. True Grace: The Life and Times of an American Princess, page 220.

Page 182: Raynauds lent Stacey chicken coop: Interview with Alain Raynaud, July 19, 2011.

Page 185: Stacey nonchalantly offered visitors a tour: Interview with Doug Wright, March 16, 2011.

Page 185: Stacey still decorated homes in the United States: Hampton. Legendary Decorators of the Twentieth Century, pages 183–195.

Page 189: Buatta recalled Stacey: Interview with Mario Buatta, July 2, 2011.

CHAPTER ELEVEN

Page 191: Stacey advised Alain Raynaud to work when inspired: Interview with Alain Raynaud, July 19, 2011.

Page 193: Balenciaga closed his fashion house when he thought elegant fashion was no longer in demand: http://www.ornamentmagazine.com/backissues/backissue_34_4_Balenciaga.php. Tamara W. Hill, "Cristóbal Balenciaga, Fashion as Refined Art." Retrieved January 21, 2013.

Page 193: It was time for Stacey to enjoy life, and he could still travel to France: Interview with Anne Cheney Zinsser, March 1, 2011.

Page 193: Stacey enjoyed gardening: Interview with Mary Ann Lyons, June 30, 2011.

Page 193: In New York, Stacey walked twenty blocks each day: Interview with Mary Ann Lyons, June 30, 2011.

Page 193: Stacey's apartment was filled with smoke: Interview with Margaretta Davison, June 17, 2011.

Page 193: Stacey did the New York Times crossword puzzle: Interview with Anne Cheney Zinsser, March 1, 2011.

Pages 193-194: Stacey's pastimes: Interview with Mary Ann Lyons, June 30, 2011.

Page 194: Stacey was planning a trip to France: Interview with Anne Cheney Zinsser, March 1, 2011.

Page 194: Stacey's behavior in his apartment building: Interview with Mary Ann Lyons, June 30, 2011.

Page 194: "Monaco is doing very well and 1989 was the forty year mark for me being at the helm! Makes me feel VERY old!!": New Year's 1990 note from Prince Rainier to Stacey.

Page 194: "Why, it didn't really hurt us": Interview with Mary Ann Lyons, June 30, 2011.

Page 194: Stacey's relationship with cats: Interview with Anne Cheney Zinsser, March 1, 2011.

Page 194: Stacey's relationship with caretaker's children: Interview with Alain Raynaud, July 19, 2011.

Page 194: Stacey was an entertaining conversationalist: interview with Peter Duchin, February 14, 2013; Hampton. Legendary Decorators of the Twentieth Century, page 186.

Page 194: Stacey relished telling stories: Eulogy for George Stacey, given by John Humpstone.

Page 194: Visits to Stacey's apartment: Interview with Doug Wright, March 16, 2011.

Page 194: Stacey's dining companions: Interview with Anne Cheney Zinsser, March 1, 2011.

Page 194: Stacey's cars: Interview with Katusha Davison, March 2, 2011.

Page 194: Stacey would show up to talk and followed the construction of a new house on the property: Interview with Harry and Margaretta Davison, June 17, 2011.

Page 194: Stacey disliked the changes to the Octagon House: Interview with Katusha Davison, March 2, 2011.

Page 194: Stacey continued to play croquet: Interview with Harry and Margaretta Davison, June 17, 2011.

Page 194: Members of the Davison family were waiting for him to move out of the squash court: Interview with Anne Cheney Zinsser, March 1, 2011.

Page 194: Stacey's driving grew erratic: Interview with Anne Cheney Zinsser, March 1, 2011.

Page 198: Stacey continued to socialize: Interview with Mary Ann Lyons, June 30, 2011.

Page 198: Mrs. Frank Wyman reminisced about a Stacey-decorated apartment: Interview with Mark and Diana Jacoby, December 22, 2012.

Page 198: Stacey was buried in Davison family plot: Interview with Anne Cheney Zinsser, March 1, 2011.

Acknowledgments

The journey of piecing together another life is a long, tessellated, and wonderful one. I could never have recomposed George Stacey—at the beginning a fragmented puzzle, disparate, mysterious, and daunting—without the generosity and support of many. I regret that space restrictions allow me only to mention a very few of a great many.

My deepest thanks to the extended Davison-Cheney clan, who were the point of departure for this journey: Anne Cheney Zinsser, Katusha Davison, Harry and Margaretta Davison, Peter von Ziegesar, Hali Lee, Lisa Tripp, and Doug Wright all gave graciously of their knowledge and time in my pursuit of George Stacey. James Davison helped me probe Stacey's soul. If it hadn't been for Lee Spilberg of the New York Public Library, who helped me initially locate Anne Zinsser, this book would have been a very truncated story indeed.

The resources and support provided to me in the Milstein Division, the Brooke Russell Astor Reading Room, and the Manuscript and Archives Division of the New York Public Library were invaluable. Gratitude, too, to Jennifer Cohlman at the Cooper-Hewitt National Design Museum and Library, Phyllis Harbinger and Lana Bittman of the Fashion Institute of Technology library, Jenny Swadosh at the Kellen Design Archives at Parsons The New School for Design, as well as the Library of Congress, Sterling Memorial Library at Yale, the New York State Archives, the Frick Art Reference Library, and the British Library.

I so appreciate the thoughtful research provided for me by Anne Kilheffer, formerly research librarian at the Stratford Library in Connecticut—you went above the call of duty to share insights and geography with me—as well as Allen Jennings of the Union Cemetery Association of Stratford, Carol Lovell and Gloria Duggan at the Stratford Historical Society, and the records office in Stratford Town Hall. Thanks to all of you, the collage of Stacey's family and early years came into sharp focus.

A delightful crew in Paris were invaluable in tracing Stacey's transatlantic footsteps: Thomas Michael Gunther, Susan Train, Jim Davison, Stephen Kirschenbaum, Charles Sevigny, Alain, Marie-Francoise, and Sophie Raynaud were boon companions, intrepid researchers, and now great friends. The Labriffe family and their trusty deputy, Armelle Lassalle, opened the Château de Neuville and its calm wonders to me. Landscape designer Christian Duvernois introduced me to Caroline Doucet and Jean-Michel Magis in Chambourcy, who made the magical Désert de Retz similarly accessible. In Monaco, Thomas Fouilleron of the Royal Archives and Heather Cohane were hospitable and helpful. A callout, too, to the wonderfully efficient Peggy Benkard, who got me across the ocean multiple times and set me up with perhaps the most scholarly driver imaginable.

I am forever indebted to those who knew Stacey and shared their stories: Mario Buatta, Betty Sherrill, Tony Victoria, Albert Hadley, Mel Dwork, Jeremiah Goodman, Pauline Metcalf, and Peter Duchin added nuance to my understanding. Descendants of Stacey clients vividly added insights and anecdotes to reconstitute a human being with all his shades, mysteries, and quirks. Alida Morgan and Wendy Goodman offered wonderful memories of the Harriman houses. Thanks to Sofia Blanchard, I was able to speak with Geoffrey Isles, Philip Isles, Jill Blanchard, and Tina Barney, who vividly described the apartment and house of Mr. and Mrs. Philip Isles. Alex and Lisa Immordino Vreeland and Laura Duarte Gómez were providential in their sharing of Vreeland photos. Rochelle and Robert Levy had knowledge that I could have never replicated. Mary Ann Lyons and Stephen McConnell of the Dorchester shared colorful and valuable memories of Stacey late in life. Hans van Nes Jr. brought his father alive to me, while Frederic Papert and Alison de Lima Greene painted a picture of Helen Marshall that fully justified Stacey's lifelong captivation. Robert R. Clark, PhD, helped interpret the details of Stacey's army record. Ed Landry connected me with Jess Morgan.

Design colleagues Nicky Haslam, Thomas Britt, Luis Rey, Tom Buckley, Susan Crater, Mary Jane Pool, Charlotte Moss, Pamela Banker, Christopher Spitzmiller, Gil Shafer, and Matthew White and dealers Bernd Goeckler, Silvanus Shaw, Katja Hirche, David Reitner, David Duncan, Mark and Diana Jacoby, Etheleen Staley, John Harvey, and Leon Dalva were excellent on details. Will Russell of Christie's, I thank you for much assistance on many levels. Others were always there for direction, insight, and experience: Hugo Vickers, Christopher Petkanas, Adam Lewis, Sian Ballen, David Patrick Columbia, Holly Brubach, Evelyn Tompkins, Philip Reeser, Craig Fitt, Bruce Shostak, David and Elizabeth Mandy, Duane Hampton, and Amy Fine Collins.

Conjuring research into a bound book could only have happened with the early insights of Suzanne Slesin, Cheryl Hurley, and Fredrica Friedman. Rob McQuilkin, my undying gratitude and affection for everything you have done on this project as agent and dear friend. Kathleen Jayes, I have loved your poise and insights at every turn, and thank you most of all for your interest in Stacey. Natalie Danford, it was a joy to read your elegant and erudite copyedits. Sandy Gilbert and Florence de Dampierre, you make the best cheerleaders. Pam Sommers and Jessica Napp were fabulous professionals. Lynn Goldberg and Angela Baggetta added their savvy and discerning refinement to the project. Susi Oberhelman, I can never tell you how brilliant you are at what you do. Charles Miers, my gratitude that you are at the helm of Rizzoli.

My family, friends, clients, and staff are at the core of my life and in every way made this book a practical venture for me. I of course thank my mother for everything! Missie Fahey, your industry acumen, experience, taste, and lovely personality crossed my path at just the right time. John Watts, *mille fois merci* for the cool sounding board, the dinners, and the respite. Big bouquets to Mario Buatta for planting the idea of the book and to Emily Eerdmans for wisdom provided along the way. Thong, thank you for believing in the endless possibilities.

My heartfelt thanks.

Photography/Illustration Credits

Courtesy of the Cecil Beaton Studio Archive at Sotheby's: Page 72. **Mita Corsini Bland:** Page 124–125. **The Bridgeman Art Library:** Page 16: Here the French are fighting, detail from the Bayeux Tapestry, before 1082 (wool embroidery on linen), French School, (11th century) / Musée de la Tapisserie, Bayeux, France / The Bridgeman Art Library. Page 26: Coffee, 1916 (oil on canvas), Matisse, Henri (1869–1954) / Detroit Institute of Arts, USA / Bequest of Robert H. Tannahill / © 2013 Succession H. Matisse /Artists Rights Society (ARS), New York. File source: Bridgeman Art Library. Page 27: Nijinsky's Faun Costume in 'L'Apres Midi d'un Faune' by Claude Debussy (1862–1918) from the front cover of the programme for the 7th season of the 'Ballets Russes', 1912 (colour litho), Bakst, Leon (1866–1924) / Bibliotheque des Arts Decoratifs, Paris, France / Archives Charmet / The Bridgeman Art Library. Page 60: Fallingwater, 1936 (photo), Wright, Frank Lloyd (1867–1959) / Mill Run, Pennsylvania, USA / © Boltin Picture Library / The Bridgeman Art Library. Page 61: Syrie Maugham's Drawing Room at 213 King's Road, Chelsea. Appearing in The Studio Feb 1933, colour print /The Stapleton Collection / The Bridgeman Art Library. **Bruce Buck:** page 10. **Carrier and Company Interiors Ltd., Mara Miller and Jesse Carrier:** Page 202. © **Christie's Images Limited:** Page 205: Photos 1–6. 8–9: 1994: Photo 7: 1999. © **Henry Clarke, Galliera, Paris, ADAGP, 2012:** Page 172. **Patrick Cline/Lonny.com:** Page 198. **Condé Nast:** Pages 5,136: Martin/*Vogue;* ©Condé Nast. Page 35: Payne/*House & Garden;* © Condé Nast. Page 37: Cassidy/*House & Garden;* © Condé Nast. Page 41: The 3/*Vogue;* ©Condé Nast. Pages 42, 43: *House & Garden;* © Condé Nast. Pages 52, 97: Beaton/ *Vogue;* © Condé Nast. Pages 55, 56–57: Van Nes/*House & Garden;* © Condé Nast. Pages 98, 99, 100: Zerbe/*Vogue;* © Condé Nast. Page 101: Leonard/*House & Garden;* © Condé Nast. Pages 102, 109,118, 119, 128, 132, 195: Rawlings/*Vogue;* © Condé Nast. Page 145: Rawlings/ *House & Garden;* © Condé Nast. Pages 105, 106–107, 122, 126–127, 134–135, 137, 138: Balkin/*Vogue;* © Condé Nast. Pages 112, 116: Walker/*House & Garden;* © Condé Nast. Pages 114, 117, 129, 130–131: Kertesz/*House & Garden;* © Condé Nast. Page 115: Gottscho-Schleisner/ *House & Garden;* © Condé Nast. Page 146: Horst/*House & Garden;* © Condé Nast. Page 147: Heillmann/*Vogue;* © Condé Nast. Page 172: Originally published in *Vogue,* Condé Nast Publications. Page 197: Saylor/Architectural Digest © Condé Nast. **Corbis:** Page 18–19: © Kelly-Mooney Photography/Corbis. Page 54: © SuperStock/Corbis. Page 103: Horst ©Condé Nast Archive/Corbis. Page 160, 183: © Norman Parkinson/Sygma/ Corbis. **Harald Haliday Costain.** Page 140–141,144 (originally published in *Town & Country,* a publication of Hearst Communications, Inc.) **Louise Dahl-Wolfe Archive:** Page 70, 71, 76–77, 80, 81, 86, 87, 90, 91: Posthumous digital reproduction from original negative; Louise Dahl-Wolfe Archive, Center for Creative Photography © 1989 Arizona Board of Regents. Page 77, 93: Collection Center for Creative Photography, University of Arizona©1989 Arizona Board of Regents. **Photograph by Anthony Denney;** originally published in *Vogue,* Condé Nast Publications**:** Page 150. **Miriam Ellner:** Page 201. **Pieter Estersohn:** Page 203. **Dessin Fournir Collections**: Pages 50, 51. **Scott Frances/OTTO;** originally published in *Architectural Digest,* Conde Nast Publications**:** page 9. **Photographs by Henry S. Fullerton, 3rd and text by Katherine Tweed** from *The Finest Rooms By America's Great Decorators,* edited by Katherine Tweed, copyright © 1964 by The Viking Press. Used by permission of Viking Penguin, a division of Penguin Group (USA) LLC.: Page 163, 189. **Ava Gardner TM is a trademark of the Ava Gardner Trust. www.AvaGardner.com.** Published in Architectural Digest: Page 181. **Getty Archives:** Page 17: Hulton Archive Staff/Hulton Archive/Getty Images. Page 20: Apic/Hulton Archive/Getty Images. Page 48: General Photographic Agency/Hulton Archive /Getty Images. Page 62: Clarence Sinclair Bull/Moviepix/Getty Images. Page 66: Walter Sanders/Time & Life Pictures/Getty Images. Page 96: MPI/Archive Images/Getty Images. Page 158: A787/Gamma-Rapho/Getty Images. Page 164: Dmitri Kessel/Time & Life Pictures/ Getty Images. **Mark Hampton:** pages 12, 13, 184, courtesy of Duane Hampton. *Harper's Bazaar,* **a publication of Hearst Communications, Inc.:** Page 110. © Estate of Horst P. Horst / Art + Commerce: Page 73. **Photograph by George Hoyningen-Huene;** ©Horst—Courtesy Staley Wise Gallery, New York City: page 3. **Illustrations John C. Hulse, Sr.:** Page 142, 143 (originally published in *Town & Country,* a publication of Hearst Communications, Inc.). **Photograph: Thibault Jeanson:** Page 199. **Kern Studio:** Page 155. **Laurie Lambrecht:** Page 200. **Library of Congress:** Page 152: Library of Congress, Prints and Photographs Division, Gottscho-Schleisner Collection LC-G613-73350. Page 153: Library of Congress, Prints and Photographs Division, Gottscho-Schleisner Collection LC-G613-73359. Page 154: Library of Congress, Prints and Photographs Division, Gottscho-Schleisner Collection LC-G613-733601. Page 156: Library of Congress, Prints and Photographs Division, Gottscho-Schleisner Collection LC-G613-73361. Page 157: Library of Congress, Prints and Photographs Division, Gottscho-Schleisner Collection LC-G613-73362. © **Fred Lyon:** Page 196. © **Estate of George Platt Lynes:** Page 67, 68–69. © **Katy McCormick:** Page 192–193. **The Metropolitan Museum of Art;** Photograph by Michael Fredericks; Copy Photograph—The Metropolitan Museum of Art: Page 79. **Courtesy National Gallery of Art, Washington:** Page 108. © **Archives du Palais Princier (Monaco)** —G. Luci: Page 159; 161. **Zachary Jean Paradis:** Page 123. **Alain Perceval:** Page 167. **Wilbur Pippin, courtesy of the late Albert Hadley:** Page 178. **Parsons School of Design Alumni Association records,** Kellen Design Archives, Parsons, The New School for Design, New York, New York: Pages 30, 31, 32, 33. **George Stacey personal papers:** pages 1, 6, 21 , 22, 32, 36,40,44, 45,49 (photo by Hans van Nes), 78, 111,133, pages 168 –171 (photos by B. Boucher), 174 (attributed to Henry Clarke), 175,182. © **Benoit Teillet:** Pages 186–187, 187. *Town & Country,* **a publication of Hearst Communications, Inc.:** Pages 54, 58, 59, 84, 85, 88: photo by Hans van Nes. **Courtesy of the Diana Vreeland Estate:** Page 74. **Courtesy of Doug Wright (painting by George Stacey):** Page 113. **Courtesy of Anne Cheney Zinsser:** pages 23, 24, and 25 (photographs by Tom Leonard); page 53.

Index

About the Author

Maureen Footer holds degrees from Wellesley College and Columbia University and studied French eighteenth century decorative arts and design at the Ecole du Louvre in Paris. She worked at McMillen Inc. and Molyneux Studio before establishing her own design firm in New York City.

First published in the United States of America in 2014
by Rizzoli International Publications, Inc. | 300 Park Avenue South | New York, NY 10010 | www.rizzoliusa.com

© 2014 Maureen Footer | Foreword © 2014 Mario Buatta

Book Design: Susi Oberhelman

Distributed in the U.S. trade by Random House, New York

ISBN-13: 978-0-8478-4245-2 | Library of Congress Catalog Control Number: 2013948615

2014 2015 2016 2017 / 10 9 8 7 6 5 4 3 2 1 | Printed in China

Page 1: George Stacey began to define his own style in Paris in the 1920s. Stacey's years in France informed the cosmopolitan designs he would produce in the upcoming decades. Page 3: Using Diana Vreeland's living room designed by Stacey as a backdrop, photographer Georges Hoyningen-Huene documented fashionable clothes in fashionable settings for *Harper's Bazaar*. Page 5: Debutante of the century Brenda Frazier hired Stacey to produce jewel-box interiors to highlight her vivid beauty, but Stacey, whose work pivoted on contrast, dictated casual flower arrangements to offset the tone of studied perfection.